The Traditional Spanish Market of Santa Fe

History and Artists of 2010

The Traditional Spanish Market of Santa Fe

History and Artists of 2010

Donna Pedace

Foreword by Arthur Lopez

Sunstone Press
SANTA FE

Sunstone books may be purchased for educational, business, or sales promotional use. For information please write: Special Markets Department, Sunstone Press, P.O. Box 2321, Santa Fe, New Mexico 87504-2321.

Book and Cover design › Vicki Ahl
Body typeface › Bernard Modern Std
Printed on acid free paper

Library of Congress Cataloging-in-Publication Data

Pedace, Donna.
The Traditional Spanish Market of Santa Fe : history and artists of 2010 / by Donna Pedace ; foreword by Arthur Lopez.
p. cm.
Includes index.
ISBN 978-0-86534-821-9 (softcover : alk. paper)
1. Hispanic American art--New Mexico. 2. Spanish Market (Santa Fe, N.M.)--History. I. Title.
N6530.N6P43 2010
704.03'680789--dc23
2011020663

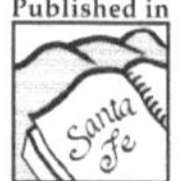

WWW.SUNSTONEPRESS.COM
SUNSTONE PRESS / POST OFFICE BOX 2321 / SANTA FE, NM 87504-2321 /USA
(505) 988-4418 / ORDERS ONLY (800) 243-5644 / FAX (505) 988-1025

Dedication

This book is dedicated to the hundreds of artists who have participated in the Traditional Spanish Market over many decades. Their creativity and hard work have preserved the traditional arts and culture of New Mexico and they daily educate the public about the importance of such preservation. It is a privilege to represent them and promote their art.

Contents

Foreword

The Traditional Spanish Market of Santa Fe is an event known throughout the world. While those hearing the name may not understand the larger purpose of the Market, the name itself brings up visions of colorful art, Latin music, and spicy Spanish food. From the first competition and exhibition by eleven artists in 1926, this event has showcased the traditional art of New Mexico and brought millions to Santa Fe.

Every July, excitement mounts around the arrival of the annual Spanish Market. The artists open their booths on Saturday morning, many still exuberant from the award ceremony held the night before where collectors and admirers alike gathered to view what the artists considered to be their best work. Market brings thousands of friends and guests to fill the Santa Fe Plaza and surrounding streets with excitement and anticipation, vying for the next unique acquisition for a private or museum collection.

As you walk around the Market, you can't help salivating over the artwork, there is a feast for the soul presented at each booth. It is this soul food that keeps visitors coming back year after year, to see the menu that is constantly changing and progressing for the visitors' impeccable taste. Each collector knows that their acquisitions at Spanish Market are sure to evoke interest and questions from those who have never had the good fortune of experiencing this momentous New Mexico celebration. Questions and comments like "Where in the world did you get that? I've never seen anything so beautiful! Where is it from?" People are often shocked when told that the art is from the Traditional Spanish Market, which is celebrating the 60th Anniversary of art, heritage, and culture of New Mexico.

Eighty-six years ago, the founders of the Spanish Colonial Arts Society created an organization that has gone on to sponsor the Market for 60 years, establish the nine-year old Museum of Spanish Colonial Art, and annually offer many educational programs to both children and adults. Their vision of preserving and promoting the traditional art forms of New Mexico has served as an inspiration to thousands of artists and visitors over the years. We've come a long way since the beginning of the Society and this book is a testament to the Society members, and the artists who work to preserve the art and share it with the world.

It is an honor and a privilege to be a part of the oldest and largest juried show of Hispanic art in the United States. The Market features unique, one-of-a-kind art pieces found only in New Mexico. It showcases the craftsmanship of more than 300 local Hispanic artisans working in this rich 400-year-old tradition.

Here in the pages of this book, you will be able to read and learn more about the Society, the Museum, the Market and, most important, the artisans who are featured each year. On behalf of all the artists in the Spanish Market, I invite you to celebrate our rich history and help us secure a bright future for this remarkable tradition that is always evolving.

Come to Market, and bring your friends!

—Arthur Lopez, 2010 Spanish Market Artist Liaison Chair

Acknowledgements

As we celebrate the 60th anniversary of the Traditional Spanish Market in 2011, we thank the many volunteers who work each year to make the Market a premier event in Santa Fe. Their contributions ensure the success of the Market, and enhance our ability to share the wealth of talent showcased each year.

We also thank the photographers who took the majority of the artists' photos: Laura Ware, Chris Riedel, Rebecca Bradshaw, and Ana June. They captured not only the images of the artists, but their love of art.

Mary Anne Kenny, Ellen Sullivan, and Linda Muzio provided valuable editing assistance.

2010 Board Members

Lorna Ortiz Calles, Secretary
Nancy Dimit
Jan Duggan
Balbino Fernández, PhD
Maria Griego-Raby, Vice President
Bonnie Hardwick, PhD
Jack Isaac
Jim Long
E. Larry Lujan
Joseph Moure, Treasurer
Ron Rivera, President
Arlene Cisneros Sena
Frank Servas
Judy Wilson

Advisory Board:

William N. Ashbey
John Berkenfield
Ray Herrera
Barbara Carpio Hoover
Eileen Wells

Honorary Board Members:

Former Governor Bill Richardson
Marta Weigle
Nancy Meem Wirth

Staff:

Donna Pedace, Executive Director
George "Bud" Redding, Spanish Market Director, through September 2010
Robin Farwell Gavin, Senior Curator, Museum of Spanish Colonial Art
Maggie Magalnick, Spanish Market Director, from September 2010
Janella Marsh, Membership and Public Relations
Linda Muzio, Education
Iris Espinoza, Security and Facilities
Theresa Gallegos, Admissions and Gift Shop
Jaime Ferrer, Admissions and Gift Shop
Jann Phillips, Bookkeeping
Bill Field, Design Consultant

The Spanish Colonial Arts Society

As early as 1913, the Society for the Revival of Spanish Arts and later, the Society for the Restoration and Preservation of Spanish Mission Churches of New Mexico, were collecting traditional New Mexico art. Both organizations were the precursors when, on October 29, 1929, author Mary Austin and artist and author Frank G. Applegate, along with a group of friends and collectors, officially founded the Spanish Colonial Arts Society. The records differ on the names of the original founders but most seemed to have also served on the Board of Trustees. The Board included Mary Austin, Frank G. Applegate, Mrs. A.S. Alvord, George M. Bloom, Leonora S. M. Curtin, Sen. Bronson M. Cutting, Archbishop Daeger, Andrew Dasburg, John D. De Huff, Margretta A. Dietrich, Alice Corbin Henderson, Mrs. Elon Hooker, John Gaw Meem, Frank E. Mera, Benigno Muniz, Mrs. Alice Clark Myers, Sheldon Parsons, Dr. Francis I. Proctor, Herman Schweizer, Mary Cabot Wheelwright, and Martha E. White. Mary Austin was elected as the first chairman.

Other names associated with the Society in its very early years included: Mrs. Ruth Laughlin Alexander, Mr. and Mrs. Gerald Cassidy, Dr. Kenneth Chapman, Miss Leonora Curtin, Mrs. Lois Field, Mr. and Mrs. Cyrus McCormick, George McCrossen, Mrs. Preston McCrossen, Mrs. Marie Robinson, artist H. Cady Wells, and others interested in preserving Spanish heritage and culture. Its original purpose, as set forth in the certificate of incorporation, was: "To encourage and promote Spanish Colonial Arts, to preserve and revive interest therein, to collect and display these arts and crafts, to promote and maintain suitable housing for such collections, to educate the public and the members of this corporation especially in the kind and qualities of the Spanish Colonial Arts and their meaning in the cultural life of Colonial times in New Mexico, and the relationship of other material from other Spanish colonies and from Spain as seen in the light of history and of art." The original mission of the Society was to "Preserve and revive the Spanish Colonial art of every character."

Three years earlier, on May 18, 1926, author and activist Mary Austin sent a letter to *The Santa Fe New Mexican* announcing the first competition designed to foster the renewal of Spanish Colonial arts among local people. Her letter states:

> During the winter of 1918, when I was traveling in New Mexico, especially in Santa Fe and Taos counties, making a survey of the Spanish-speaking population for the Americanization Study under the Carnegie Foundation, I became acquainted with one of the native resources of the state which was then, and is still, practically unworked, a resource from which not only financial returns could be expected, but good repute, the respect and admiration of the world outside. I mean the resources of artistic capacity resident in our Spanish colonial population. And a great many people have thought as I did eight years ago, that the capacity to produce work of equal value remains with the Spanish-speaking population, and could, with very little encouragement become a pleasant and profitable activity among them. Through the interest and generosity of Mrs. Elon Hooker of New York, and Miss Mary Wheelwright of Boston and Alcalde, I am able to announce a prize competition for modern examples of Spanish colonial arts and crafts, open to any native New Mexican of Spanish descent.

The letter went on to request volunteers to assist with that first competition and exhibition of Hispanic art. From that simple beginning emerged an organization that has been crucial to preserving and promoting Hispanic art for more than 85 years.

The initial 1926 Spanish Market was an effort by this small group to support and promote the local New Mexican art forms, and the men and women who created them.

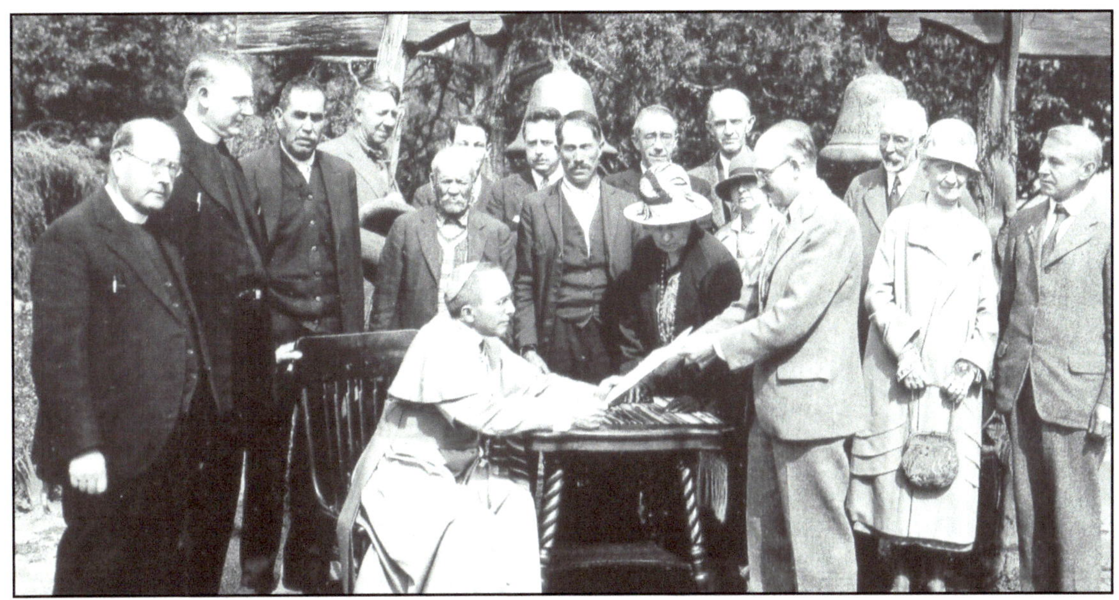

John Gaw Meem presenting the deed for El Santuario de Chimayo to Archbishop Albert T. Daeger in the latter's garden, October 15, 1929. Others in attendance: Paul A. F. Walter, Mrs. John Robinson of Sunmount, Dr. Francis Proctor, Alice Corbin Henderson, unknown man, E. Dana Johnson, Mary Austin, Gustave Baumann, Marcos Chavez, Daniel T. Kelly, Judge Charles Fahy, Jose Chavez, Frank Applegate, Victor Ortega, Bishop Espalage, and Father Salvatore Gene of Santa Cruz.

On October 15, 1929, two weeks before the Society's incorporation paperwork was officially signed, the Society purchased a privately owned chapel in the village of Chimayo. The purchase price of $6000 was raised by Mary Austin and others from a private donor in the East who set the condition that he remain anonymous. The chapel was immediately given to the Archdiocese of Santa Fe and, for almost 20 years, the Society provided basic maintenance. Later, the chapel was totally refurbished and became known throughout the world as *El Santuario de Chimayo,* the Lourdes of America. Later, in 1954, the Society assisted with financing the renovation work of the old Plaza del Cerro at Chimayo.

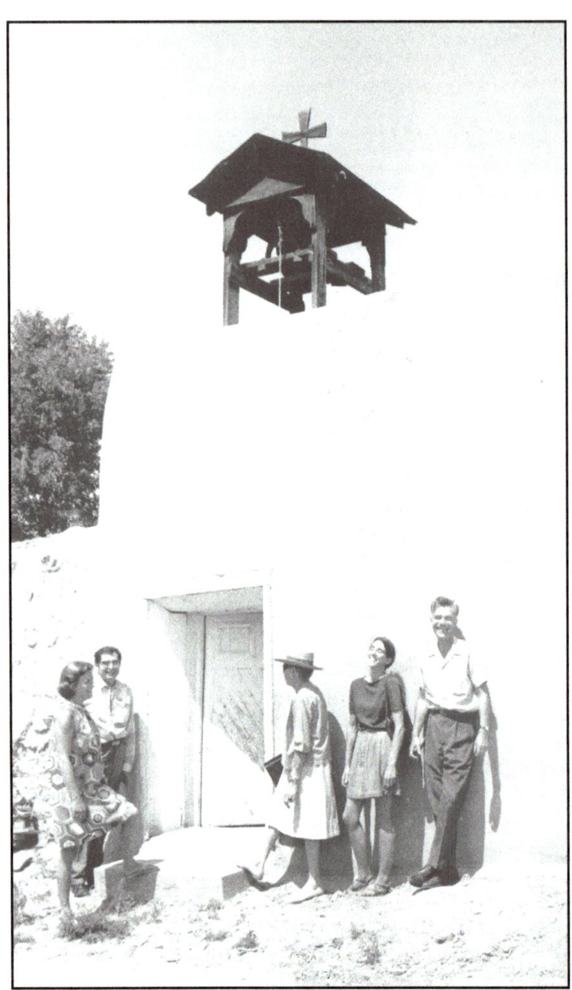

Ann Vedder, unknown, E Boyd, unknown, Alan Vedder at work on Chimayo Chapel

The second major purchase undertaken by the Society was an altar screen by 19th century master *santero* José Rafael Aragón, originally from the *Nuestra Señora del Carmen* church at Llano Quemado. The altar screen was sold to the Society by the committee in charge of church building at Llano Quemado after it had been replaced at the church by a millwork altar screen. This altar screen was loaned to the Palace of the Governors in 1929 and it remains on long-term loan, and is a popular exhibit today.

From 1930 to 1933, the Society operated The Spanish Shop at Room 39 of Sena Plaza that offered a sales inventory of the work of the Market artists. The Society also had some success in convincing galleries in the East to display the work of a few of the artists of northern New Mexico.

Frank Applegate served as curator of the collection from 1929 until his death in 1931 and the Society purchased several art items from his personal collection. Mary Austin died in 1934 and, following her death, the Society was relatively inactive during the late 1930s and through the 1940s. During these quiet years, the art previously collected was maintained in the homes of former Board members.

In 1938, the Society mounted a special exhibition of Spanish Colonial Art at the Museum of New Mexico's Palace of the Governors. The Society placed forty-eight objects at the Palace, including hide paintings, Rio Grande blankets, Mexican reboots, altar cloths, and other art objects.

In the early 1950s, the Spanish Colonial art scholar, Elizabeth Boyd White, known professionally as E Boyd, was appointed as the first curator of the newly established Spanish Colonial Arts Department at the New Mexico Museum of International Folk Art. E Boyd, along with a small group of the original founders, reinvigorated the Society and served as the curator of the Society's collection for many years. On February 14, 1952, Lois Field became interim president of the newly reactivated group. In June of that same year, Wayne L. Mauzy was elected president of the new sixteen-member Board of Trustees.

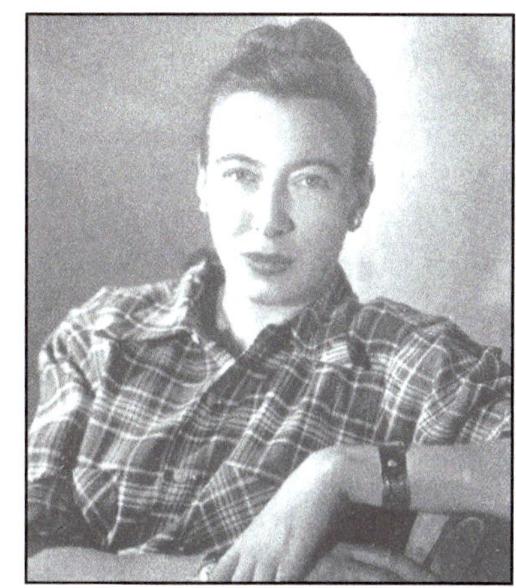

E Boyd, 1930

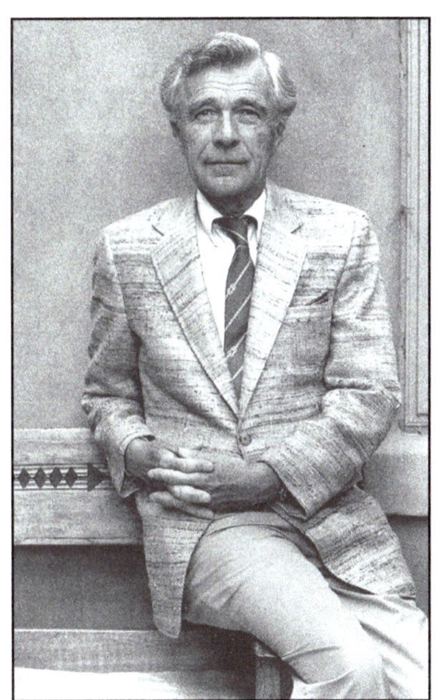

Alan Vedder

Alan C. and Ann Vedder joined the organization in the early 1950s and they remained deeply involved until their deaths in the 1990s. Alan and Ann shared the leadership of the Society with E Boyd and together they expanded and restored the collection. The first inventory of the collection was done by E Boyd and the Vedders. Over two decades, they acquired and restored hundreds of art objects and arranged several significant bequests to the collection. During those years, a

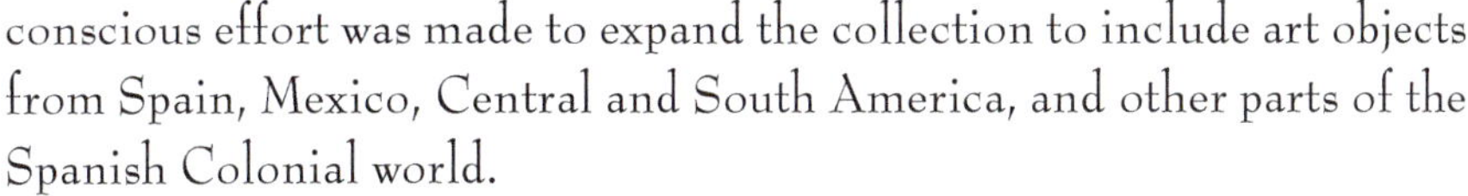

conscious effort was made to expand the collection to include art objects from Spain, Mexico, Central and South America, and other parts of the Spanish Colonial world.

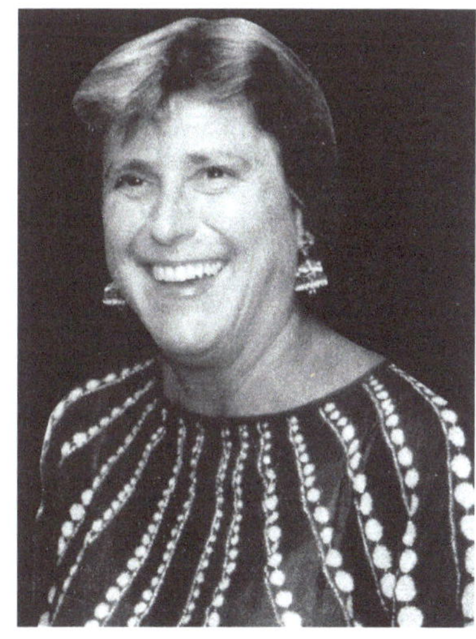

Ann Vedder

The Society reached an official agreement with the Museum of International Folk Art on May 4, 1961 to house the Society's collection until such time as the Society could build a new museum. The collection remained at the International Folk Art Museum for more than 40 years, and the Society is grateful to the state museum for preserving the collection.

In 1965, the Spanish Market was resurrected as an annual event and was held beneath the portal of the First National Bank of Santa Fe facing the Plaza. The location of the Market shifted a few times over the next several years, as the number of artists participating in the event grew. The portal of the Palace of the Governors was also used for several years.

Alan Vedder followed E Boyd as the curator of the collection after her death in 1974 and remained in that position until his death in 1989, when he was replaced by Donna Pierce, PhD. More than 70 art objects from the Society's collection were showcased in the 1989 long-term inaugural exhibition of the new Hispanic Heritage Wing at the Museum of International Folk Art.

The Society's "museum on paper" was celebrated with the 1996 publication of *Spanish New Mexico: The Spanish Colonial Arts Society Collection*, edited by Donna Pierce and Marta Weigle. The book is dedicated to the memories of Alan and Ann Vedder.

Stuart Ashman was chosen as Executive Director in 2000 and led the Society through the capital campaign and the construction work on the long hoped-for museum. In 2003, Bill Field followed Ashman as Director, and Donna Pedace was selected as Executive Director in 2010.

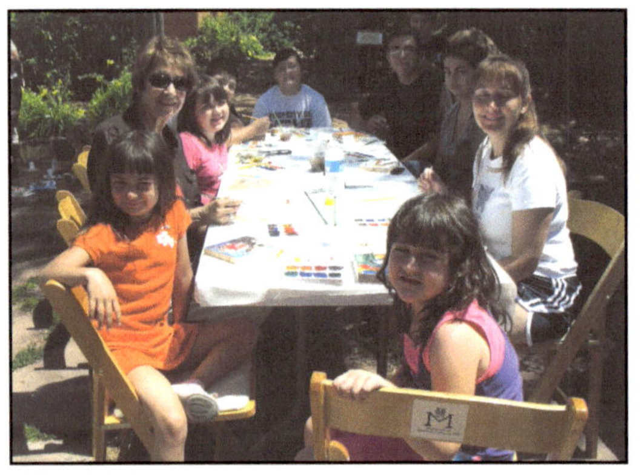

Arts Alive Workshop

The current mission of the Society is to: "Collect, preserve, and exhibit the Spanish Colonial art of New Mexico and beyond, and educate the public about its related culture and living traditions."

The Society offers art programs taught by Market artists for children in schools and at the museum. Market artists also offer art workshops for adults to learn more about the traditional arts of New Mexico and a wide range of lectures are offered covering the areas of art, history, and culture.

Traditional Spanish Market

The first Market was held in 1926 at the New Mexico Museum of Fine Art and later moved to the portal of the Palace of the Governors. By 1931, there were thirty-one cash awards given to adult artists at the Market, plus five prizes of two dollars each for the best work by local school children. The financial expectations of the artists were modest in those days as Marta Weigle reports in her book *Hispanic Arts and Ethnohistory in the Southwest:* "Celso Gallegos, an Agua Fria wood and stone carver, received 60 silver dollars from Applegate and was so astounded that he cried and attempted to kiss Applegate." Today, a single piece can sell for many hundreds or thousands of dollars.

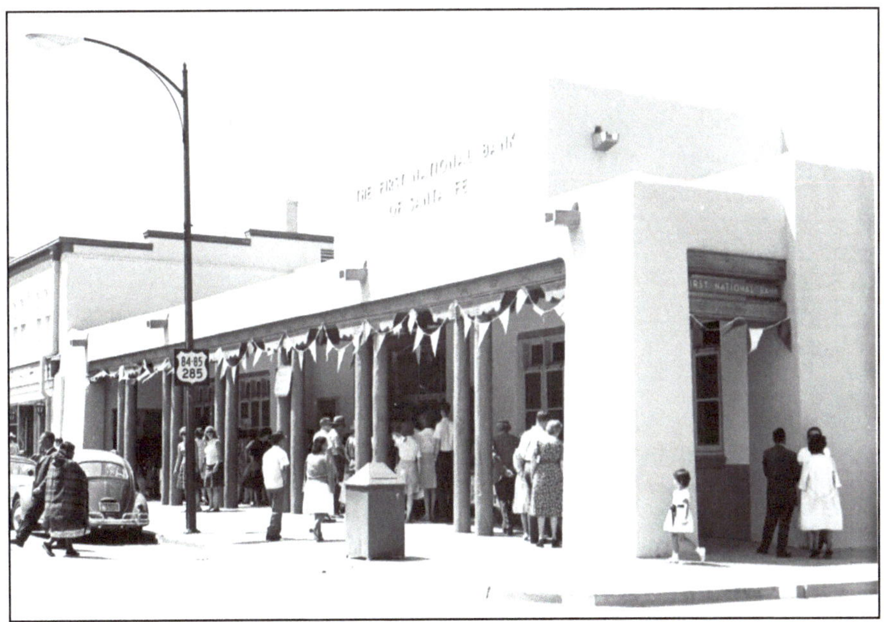

Spanish Market, 1965

The Market was not held during the Depression or World War II, but was revived in 1965 with eighteen artists exhibiting their work. A scheduling problem caused the Market to remain closed in 1966 but it resumed in 1967 and has been an annual event since that date. From 1967 until 1971, Spanish Market and Indian Market took place on the same August weekend under the portal of the First National Bank.

In the 1970s, E Boyd and Alan Vedder encouraged the artists to do in-depth research in the museum collections, both for inspiration and for historical accuracy. Several categories were added to the Spanish Market Standards as a result of that research, including Furniture, Straw Appliqué, Filigree Jewelry, *Retablos*, Weaving, Leatherwork, and Ironwork. The Society officially added the Youth Market to the annual summer Market in 1981.

In 1989, a Winter Spanish Market was established during the first full weekend in December. The Winter Market has approximately 75-100 artists who exhibit and sell their work. Thousands of residents and visitors attend the Winter Market and a tradition of purchasing holiday gifts has grown up around this Market.

Artist participation in the market increased rapidly during the 1990s. Several new categories were added including: Painted *Bultos*, *Bultos en Nicho,* Unpainted *Bultos,* and Mixed Media. Precious Metals and Tinwork became two separate categories.

The Traditional Spanish Market remains the oldest and largest juried Spanish Market in the United States. The jury process for acceptance into the Market is determined by standards that have been set by the artists themselves to ensure the quality of the work, and also to ensure that each artist understands and uses traditional methods and materials.

The Market is held annually on the last Saturday and Sunday in July, attracting from 40,000—60,000 visitors to Santa Fe. The Market offers incredible art, traditional foods, and music and dancing which add to the festive atmosphere. The Friday night before the Market is Preview Night, where sponsors and Society members have an opportunity to meet the artists and view the art that was submitted for award consideration, as well as all the award-winning pieces. On Sunday morning of Market weekend, a Market Mass is celebrated in the Cathedral with a blessing of the artists and their presented art pieces.

George "Bud" Redding was selected as the first Spanish Market Director in 1984 and he was succeeded by Deborah "Maggie" Magalnick in 2010. Thousands of artists and volunteers have worked with the staff of the Society over the years to plan and produce the annual summer and winter Markets. Their assistance has been invaluable in ensuring the success of each Market.

As the Market grew, it moved to the Plaza area and now covers not only the Plaza but also several surrounding streets. Between 250 and 300 artists annually participate in the Market each summer and there is an active Youth Market representing young artists between the ages of eight and seventeen. The 2010 Market was the 59th year that the Hispanic artists of New Mexico have exhibited and sold their art to the world.

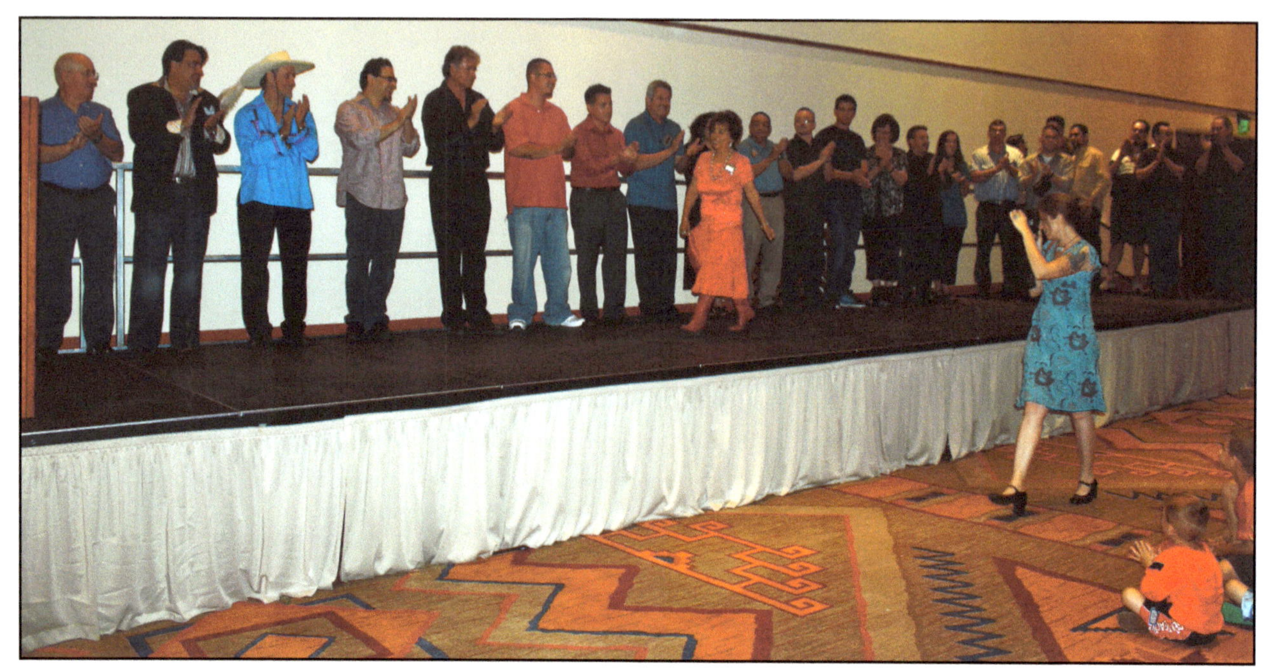

Julia Gómez accepting her Grand Prize Award for Best of Show 2010.

Artists of the 2010 Traditional Spanish Market

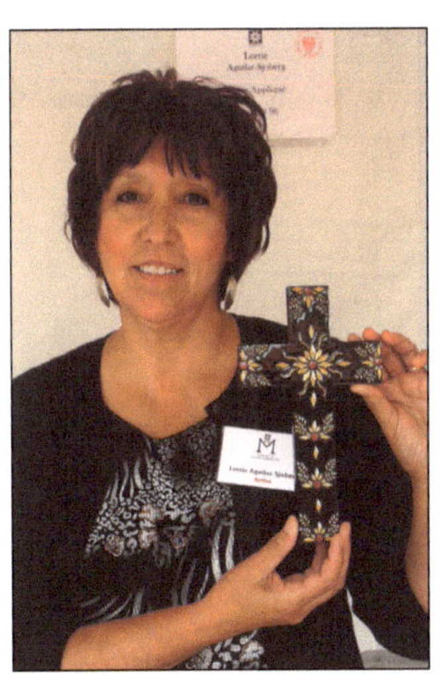

Lorrie Aguilar-Sjoberg
Art Form: Straw Appliqué
Contact: (505) 934-2326
Born in Albuquerque, New Mexico
Lives in Albuquerque, New Mexico
Juried into Spanish Market in 1996.

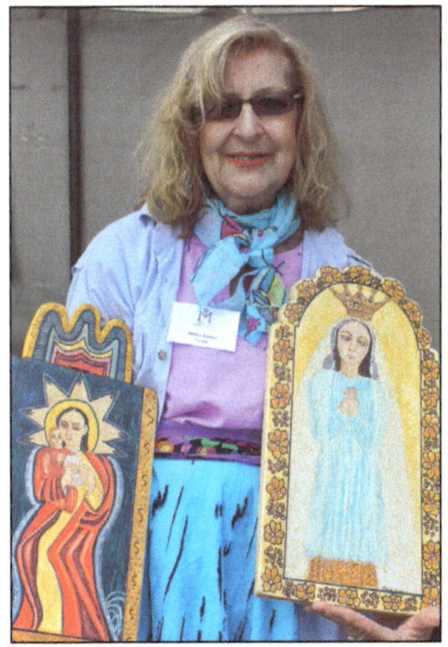

Maria Anaya-Rutkowsky
Art Form: *Retablos*
Contact: (505) 792-4922
Born in Belen, New Mexico
Lives in Albuquerque, New Mexico
Juried into Spanish Market in 2010.

Adrian A. Aragón

Art Form: *Retablos*
Contact: (505) 877-9232
Born in Albuquerque, New Mexico
Lives in Albuquerque, New Mexico
Juried into Spanish Market in 2008
Notable Award:
Spanish Market Honorable Mention and People's Choice Awards 2008.

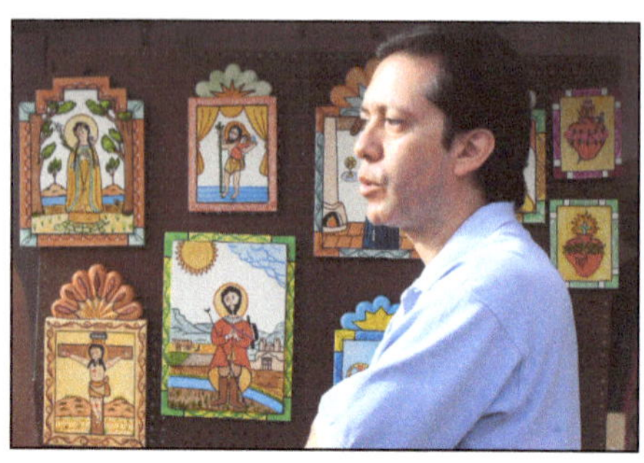

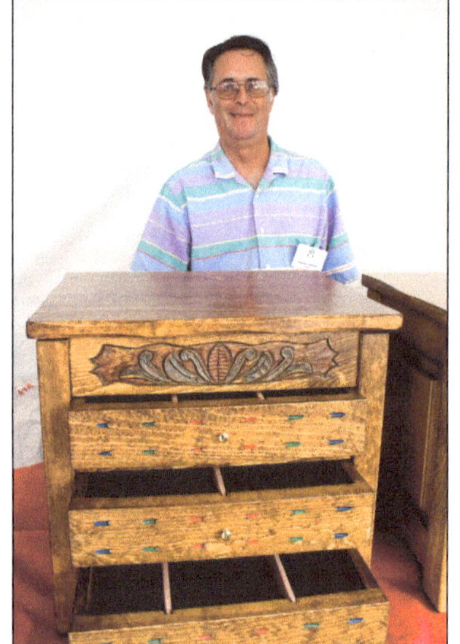

Antonio J. Archuleta

Art Form: Furniture
Contact: (575) 776-8659
Born in Taos, New Mexico
Lives in Arroyo Hondo, New Mexico
Juried into Spanish Market in 1988 and again in 1994
Notable Awards:

Spanish Market Best of Furniture 1989.
Taos Invites Taos Best of Furniture 1996 and again in 2007.
State of New Mexico Legislature and Secretary of State Certificates of Recognition.

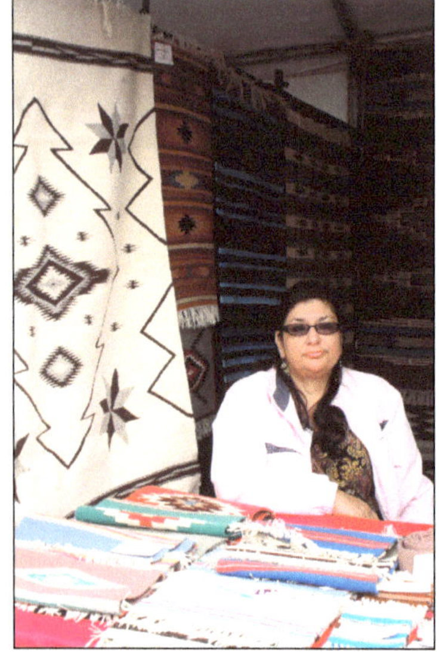

Delores Archuleta

Art Form: Weaving
Lives in Medanales, New Mexico.

Eppie Archuleta

Art Form: Weaving
Contact: (505) 685-0047
Born in Santa Cruz, New Mexico
Lives in Medanales, New Mexico
Juried into Spanish Market in 1965
Notable Awards:
Spanish Market Masters Award for Lifetime Achievement 2001.

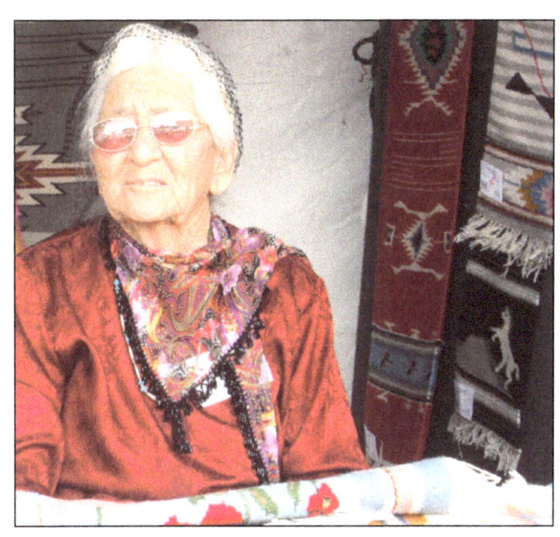

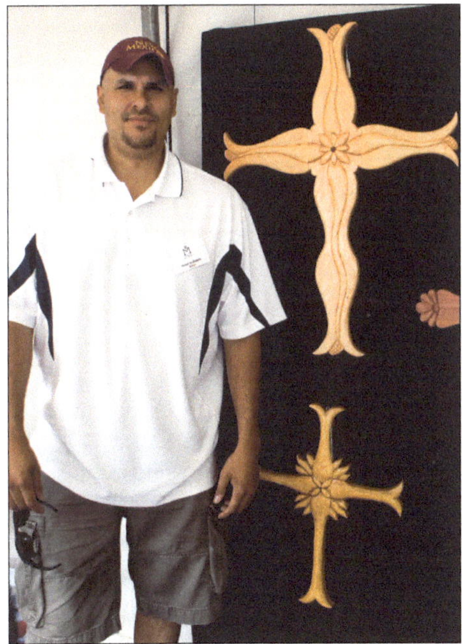

Victor Archuleta

Art Form: Furniture
Contact: (505) 747-0443
Born in Santa Fe, New Mexico
Lives in Española, New Mexico
Juried into Spanish Market in 2008
Notable Awards:

Northern New Mexico Art Show Second Place for Traditional Furniture in 2005, Best of Show in 2006, First Place in 2006. Española Valley Arts Festival First Place in Traditional Furniture in 2006, the Tim Roybal Award for Excellence in Furniture in 2007. New Mexico State Fair Third Place in Traditional Furniture in 2007.

José Armijo

Art Form(s): Painted *Bultos*, *Retablos*, Relief Carvings
Contact: (505) 753-2056
Born in Santa Fe, New Mexico
Lives in Santa Cruz, New Mexico
Juried into Spanish Market in 1997
Notable Awards:
Spanish Market E Boyd Award 2004.

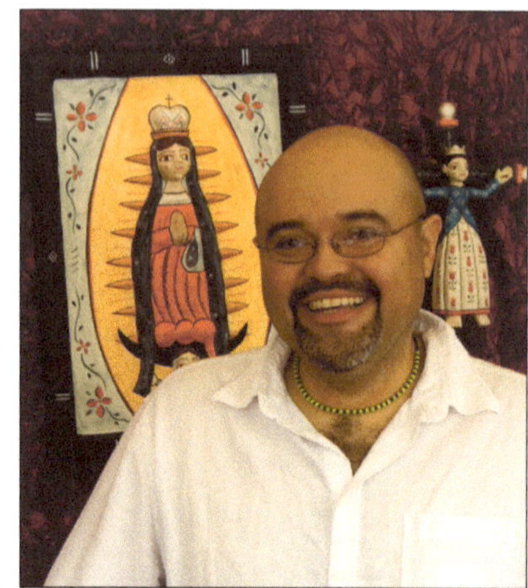

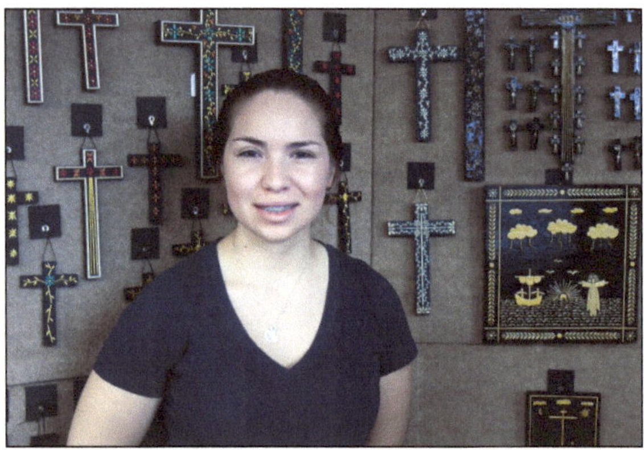

Anjelica Mariah Baca

Art Form: Straw Appliqué
Contact: (505) 321-7581
Born in Albuquerque, New Mexico
Lives in Albuquerque, New Mexico
Juried into Spanish Market in 2010.

Lawrence Baca

Art Form: Precious Metals
Contact: (505) 983-9119
Born in Santa Fe, New Mexico
Lives in Santa Fe, New Mexico
Juried into Spanish Market in 1994
Notable Awards:
Spanish Market several First and Second Place Awards in Precious Metals and Mixed Media as well as: Collaboration, E Boyd, and several Purchase Awards.
Feria Artistica Best of Show
Taylor Museum Best of Show.
City of Santa Fe Excellence in the Arts Award
Special gift to Pope John Paul II in collaboration with Arlene Cisneros Sena presented at the Vatican by Archbishop Michael Sheehan.

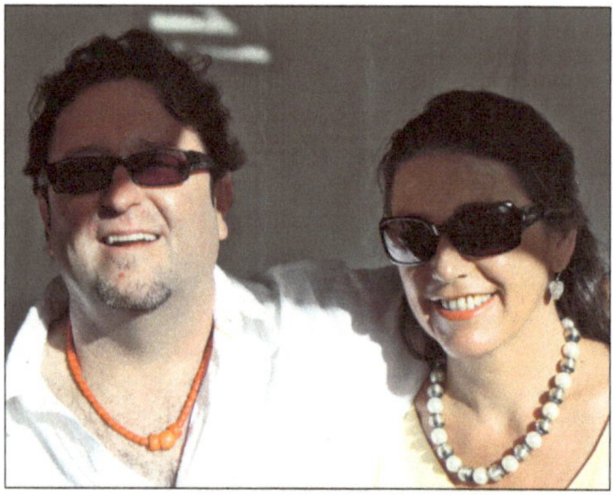

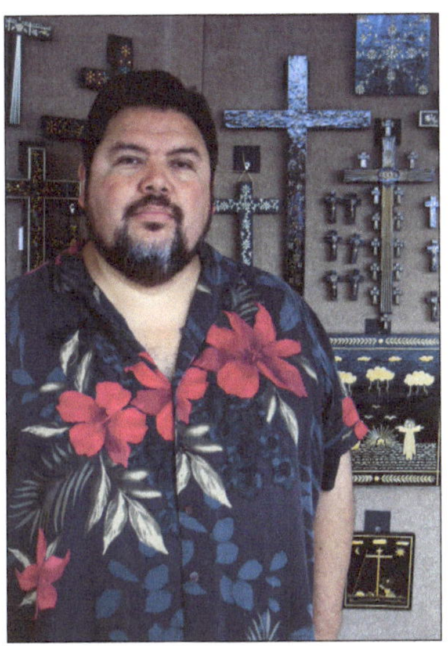

Ray Baca, Jr.

Art Form: Straw Appliqué
Contact: (505) 480-9566
Born in Lemitar, New Mexico
Lives in Albuquerque, New Mexico
Juried into Spanish Market in 2004
Notable Awards:
Spanish Market Design Award 2004.

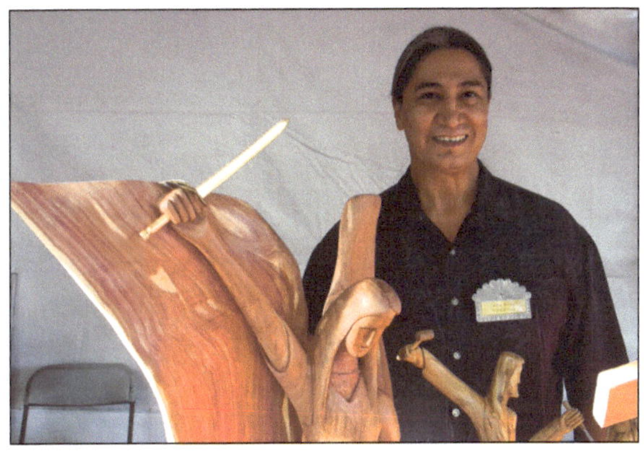

Carlos Barela

Art Form: Woodcarving
Lives in Ranchos de Taos, New Mexico

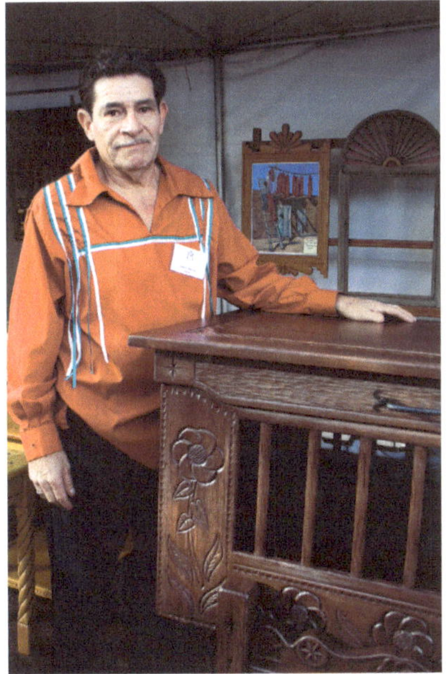

José V. Barela

Art Form: Furniture
Contact: (505) 304-2434
Born in Santa Fe, New Mexico
Lives in Albuquerque, New Mexico
Juried into Spanish Market in 1993
Notable Awards:
Española Arts Festival Second Place 1994.
New Mexico State Fair Third Place in Traditional Furniture in 1995 and 1996 and Honorable Mention in 1997.

Roberto E. Barela
Art Form: Woodcarving
Lives in Ranchos de Taos, New Mexico.

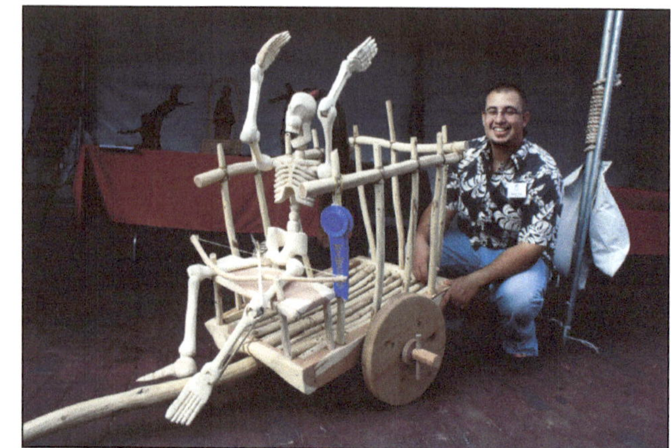

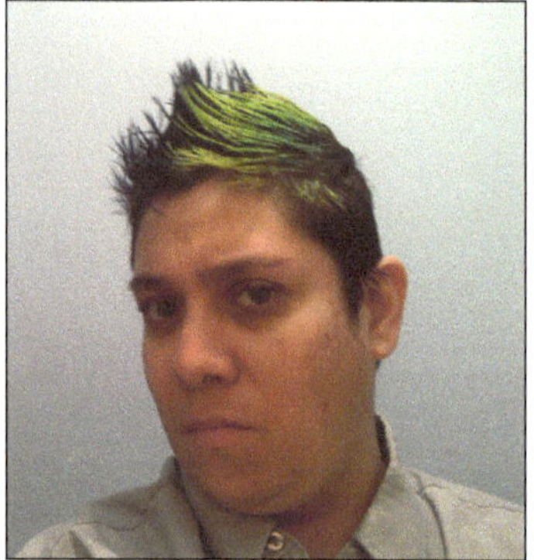

Lena Blea
Art Form:
Ramilletes
Contact: (303) 895-0142
Born in Sterling, Colorado
Lives in Denver, Colorado
Juried into Spanish Market in 2006.

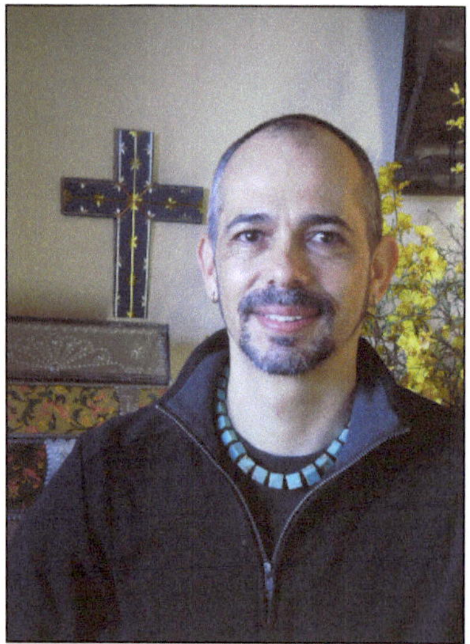

Kevin Burgess de Chávez
Art Form: Tinwork
Contact: (505) 873-3325
Born in Albuquerque, New Mexico
Lives in Albuquerque, New Mexico
Juried into Spanish Market in 2005
Notable Awards:
- Spanish Market Boeckman Award 2008 and 2009.
- New Mexico Arts & Crafts Best of Show 2006.
- New Mexico State Fair First Place 2007.
- Named Albuquerque Local Treasure 2008.

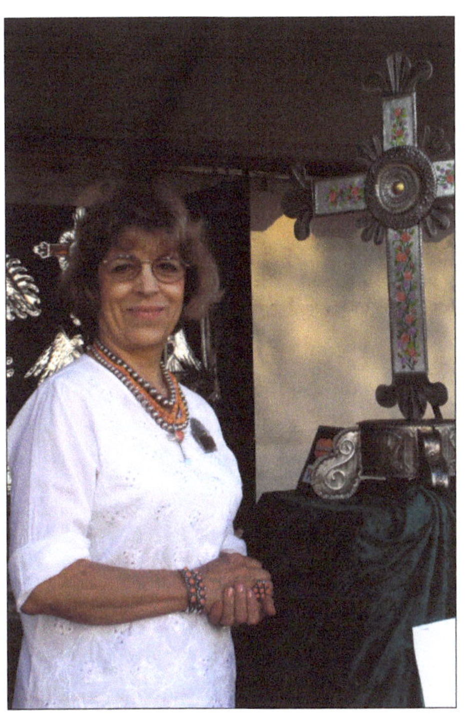

Christine Montaño Carey

Art Form(s): Tinwork, *Retablos*
Contact: (505) 438-3054
Born in Las Vegas, New Mexico
Lives in Santa Fe, New Mexico
Juried into Spanish Market in 2006
Notable Awards:

Spanish Market Winter Market People's Choice Award in 2007, El Rancho de las Golondrinas Award in 2009, and Winter Market Boeckman Award for New Direction in 2010.

Nuestra Senora de Perpetuo Socorro Second Place in 2004.

New Mexico State Fair Honorable Mention in 2004, Jerry & Sheryl Montoya Award of Excellence in 2005, Second Place in 2005, Fiesta de Colores Award and Women's Award of Excellence in 2006, First Place and Best of Show in 2007, and Honorable Mention in 2009.

Española Valley Art Festival First Place in 2007.

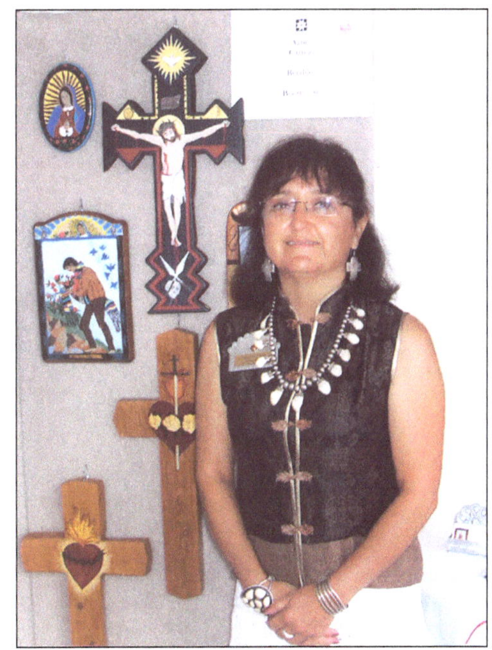

Agnes Carrejo

Art Form: *Retablos*
Contact: (505) 250-2740
Born in St. Johns, Arizona
Lives in Apache Creek, New Mexico
Juried into Spanish Market in 2008.

Vicky Carrejo

Art Form: Straw Appliqué
Contact: (505) 412-0100
Born in Reserve, New Mexico
Lives in White Rock, New Mexico
Juried into Spanish Market in 2005.

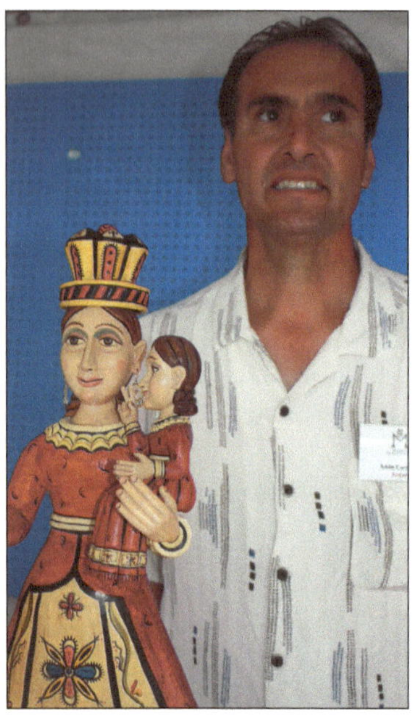

Adán Carriaga

Art Form(s): Painted *Bultos*, *Retablos*
Contact: (505) 244-0208
Born in Albuquerque, New Mexico
Lives in Albuquerque, New Mexico
Juried into Spanish Market in 2005
Notable Awards:

Spanish Market Bienvenidos Award 2005.
San Felipe de Neri Santero Market Parish Award 2002, Second Place 2003 and 2006.
New Mexico State Fair Hispanic Arts Center; St. Bernadette's Art Institute Blue Ribbon for Most Inspirational Piece 2003 and Honorable Mention 2010.
Feria Artistica Honorable Mention in 2003 and Special Recognition Award in 2004.

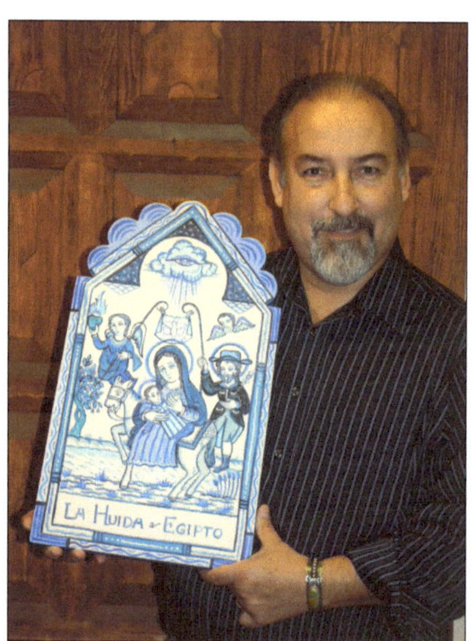

Charles M. Carrillo

Art Form(s): Painted *Bultos*, *Retablos*, Relief Carving
Contact: (505) 473-7941
Born in Albuquerque, New Mexico
Lives in Santa Fe, New Mexico
Juried into Spanish Market in 1980
Notable Awards:

Spanish Market Grand Prize for Best of Show 1990.
Archbishop's Award in 2002, New Directions Award in 2000 and 2003, Winter Market People's Choice Award in 2005, Masters Award for Lifetime Achievement and People's Choice Award in both Summer and Winter Market in 2006, Honorable Mention 2007.
The National Endowment for the Arts Heritage Fellowship Award in 2006.

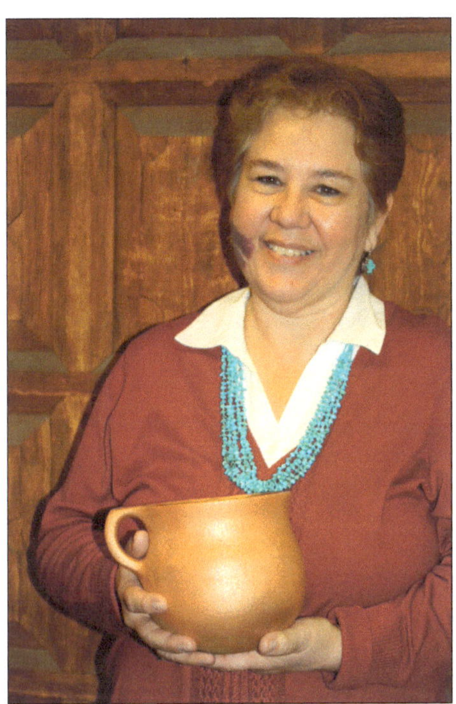

Debbie B. Carrillo

Art Form: Pottery
Contact: (505) 473-7941
Born in Abiquiu, New Mexico
Lives in Santa Fe, New Mexico
Juried into Spanish Market in 1991
Notable Awards:
Spanish Market Honorable Mention in 2002, Collaboration Award and Utilitarian Award in 2004.

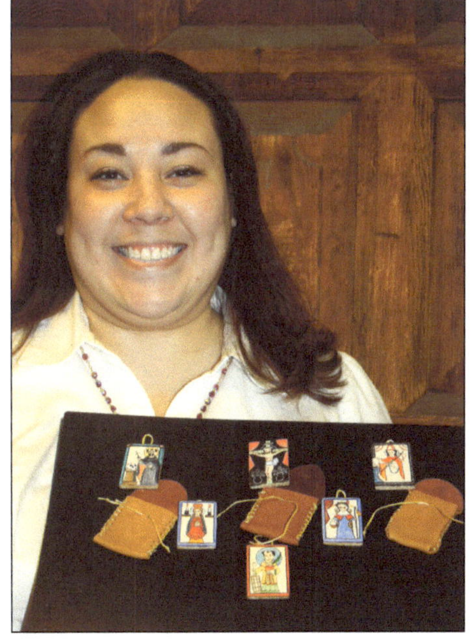

Estrellita A. Carrillo-Garcia

Art Form(s): Painted *Bultos*, *Retablos*, Ramillettes, Leatherwork
Contact: (505) 896-6866 or (505) 690-9366
Born in Albuquerque, New Mexico
Lives in Rio Rancho, New Mexico
Juried into Spanish Market in 1998
Notable Awards:
Spanish Market Second Place Altar Screens 2010.

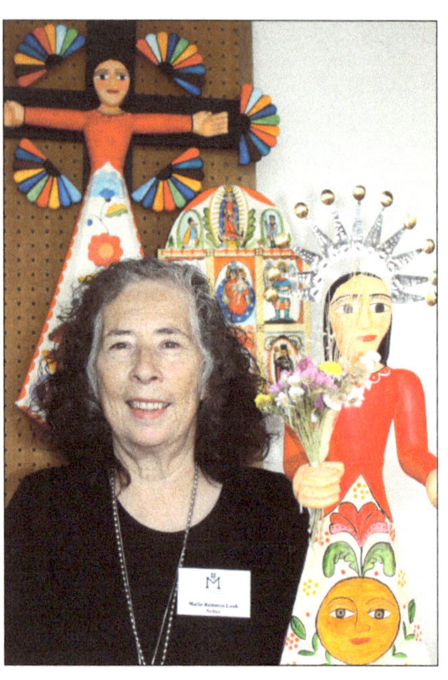

Marie Romero Cash

Art Form(s) *Retablos*, Painted *Bultos*
Contact: (505) 988-2590
Born in Santa Fe, New Mexico
Lives in Santa Fe, New Mexico
Juried into Spanish Market in 1975
Notable Awards:

Spanish Market E Boyd Award 1985, Best of Show Award 1987 and 1988, Mixed Media 1991, Master's Award for Lifetime Achievement 1992, Purchase Award and E Boyd Award 1999, Distinguished Artist Award and Market Poster Award 2000, Mixed Media and Florence Dibell Bartlett Award 2003, Boeckman New Directions Award 2004 and 2008.

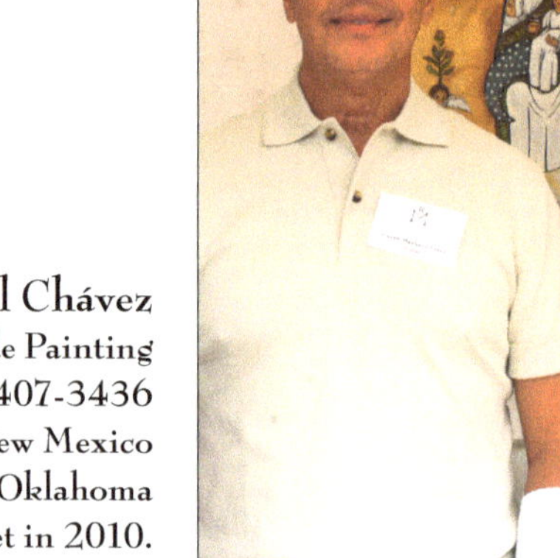

Joseph Manuel Chávez

Art Form: Hide Painting
Contact: (918) 407-3436
Born in Deming, New Mexico
Lives in Tulsa, Oklahoma
Juried into Spanish Market in 2010.

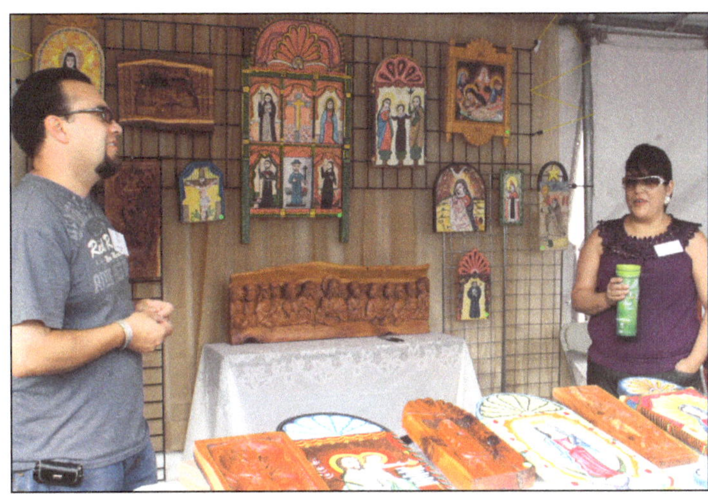

Patricio Chávez

Art Form: Relief Carving
Contact: (505) 614-7275
Born in El Paso, Texas
Lives in Chimayo, New Mexico
Juried into Spanish Market in 2008
Notable Awards:
Spanish Market Wood Relief Award 2010.

Shawna L. Chávez

Art Form: *Retablos*
Contact: (505) 614-7273
Born in Española, New Mexico
Lives in Chimayo, New Mexico
Juried into Spanish Market in 2008.

Veronica Montaño Coale

Art Form(s): Colcha, Precious Metals
Contact: (575) 588-7324
Born in Santa Fe, New Mexico
Lives in Las Nutrias near Tierra Amarilla, New Mexico
Juried into Spanish Market in 2003
Notable Awards:
Spanish Market First Place Colcha 2004, Second Place Precious Metals 2005, Honorable Mention Precious Metals 2006, First Place Precious Metals 2008 and 2010.
New Mexico State Fair First Place 2004, First and Second Place Precious Metals 2005, First Place 2006.

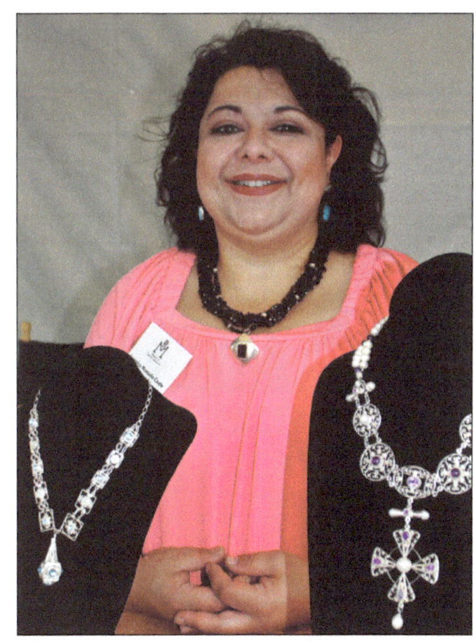

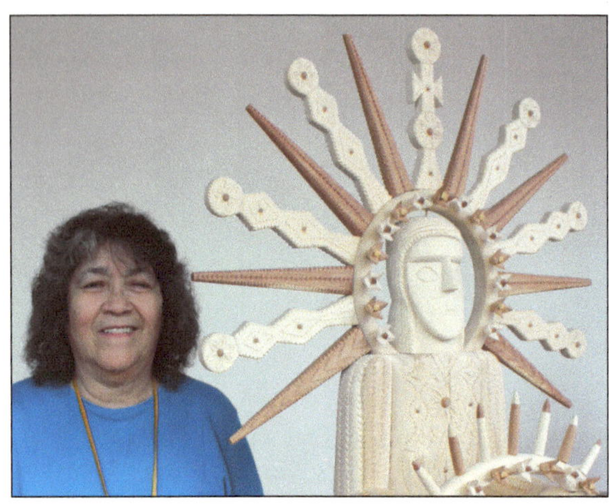

Gloria López Córdova

Art Form: Woodcarving
Contact: (505) 351-4487
Born in Córdova, New Mexico
Lives in Córdova, New Mexico
Juried into Spanish Market in 1960
Notable Awards:

Spanish Market Best of Show 1991, First Place 1992/1994/1995/1996/2001/2003/2008, Purchase Award 1993 and 2008, Leo Salazar Award First Place 2001/2004/2006/2007 and Second Place 2003 & 2005, Honorable Mention 2002, José Dolores López Award 1994/1995/1996/1997/1999/2002/2003/2006/2008, Masters Award for Lifetime Achievement 2009.
New Mexico State Fair Second Place Unpainted *Bultos* 1997.
Governor's Award for Excellence in the Arts 1983.
Woman's Award of Excellence 2001.
Denver Spanish Market Best of Show 2007.

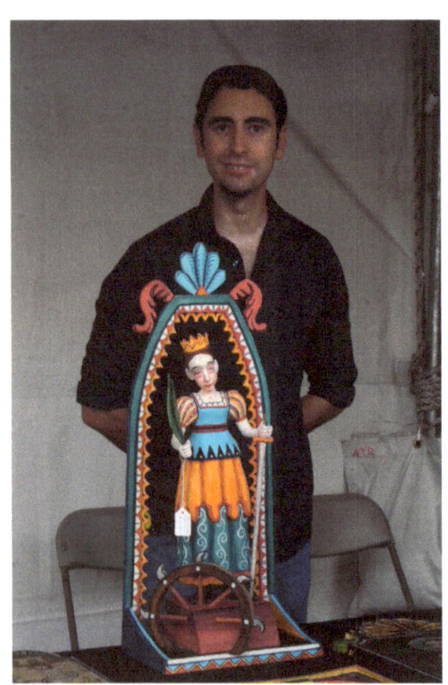

James M. Córdova

Art Form(s): Painted *Bultos*, *Retablos*, Gesso Relief
Contact: (575) 517-9121
Born in Santa Fe, New Mexico
Lives in Boulder, Colorado
Juried into Spanish Market in 1992
Notable Awards:

Spanish Market First Place *Retablos* multiple times, Hispanic Heritage Award 1993, First Place Altar Screens, First Place *Bultos* en Nicho multiple times, Archbishop's Award 1998, Second Place *Retablos* 1995, Second Place *Bultos* en Nicho 2003 and 2010,
Third Place Large *Retablos* 2010.

Lawrence Córdova

Art Form(s): Painted *Bultos, Retablos*
Contact: (505) 474-5966
Born in Santa Fe, New Mexico
Lives in Santa Fe, New Mexico
Juried into Spanish Market in 1995.

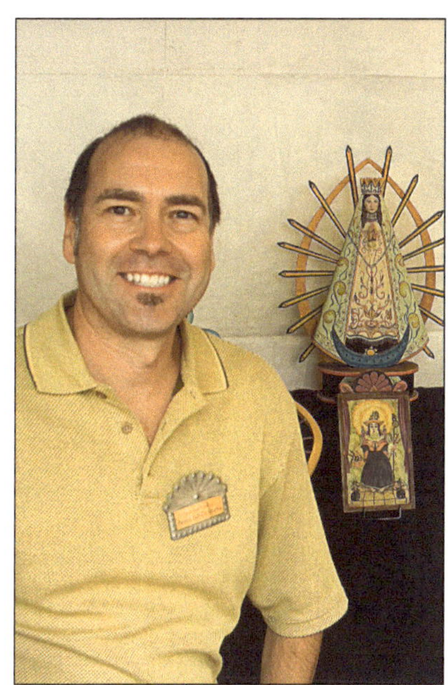

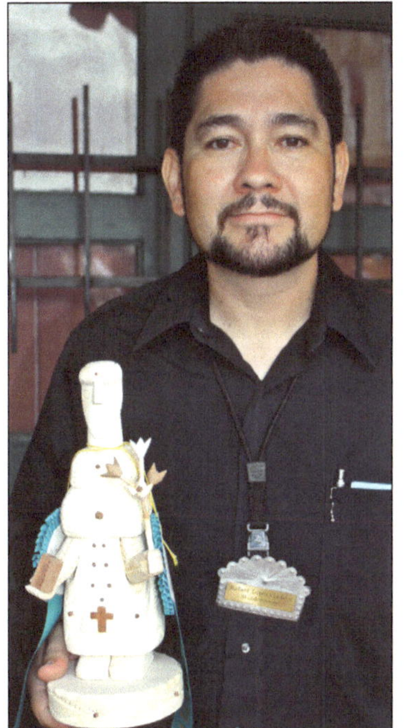

Rafael López Córdova

Art Form: Woodcarving
Contact: (505) 927-0759
Born in Española, New Mexico
Lives in Córdova, New Mexico
Juried into Spanish Market in 1986
Notable Awards:
Spanish Market Purchase Award 1992; Alan and Ann Vedder Award 1999, Multiple Awards for Honorable Mention, First Place, and the José Dolores López Award 2010. Tesoro Foundation Best of Show 1991.

Rhonda Crespin

Art Form(s): Painted *Bultos, Retablos*
Contact: (505) 328-4658
Born in Albuquerque, New Mexico
Lives in Jemez Springs, New Mexico
Juried into Spanish Market in 1992
Notable Awards:
Spanish Market Purchase Award 1994, Distinguished Artist Award 2000, First Place 2001, and Second Place, 2007. New Mexico State Fair Honorable Mention 1998.

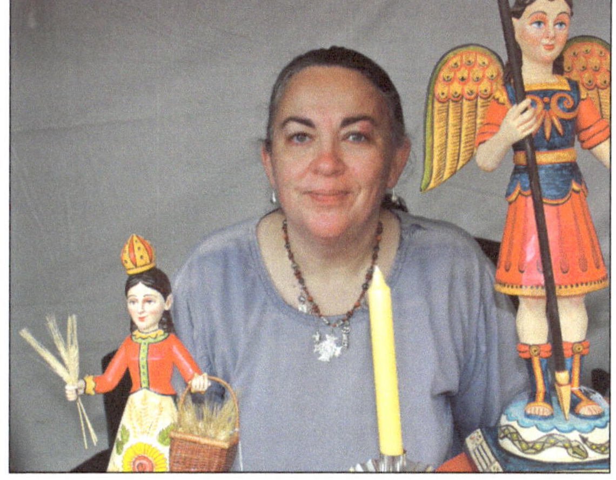

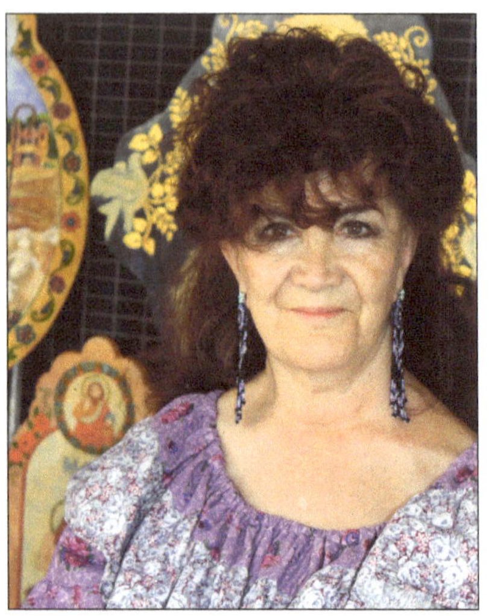

Carmelita Laura Valdes Damron

Art Form(s): *Retablos*, Tinwork
Contact: (505) 983-4033
Born in Alamosa, Colorado
Lives in Santa Fe, New Mexico
Juried into Spanish Market in 1980
Notable Awards:
Spanish Market Hispanic Heritage Award Honorable Mention 2005, Purchase Award.

J.D. Damron y Valdes

Art Form: Tinwork
Contact: (505) 424-0682
Born in Wurtzberg, Germany
Lives in Tesuque, New Mexico
Juried into Spanish Market in 1988.

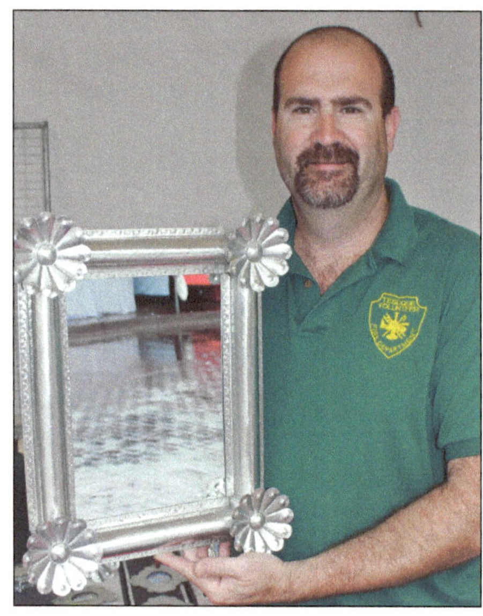

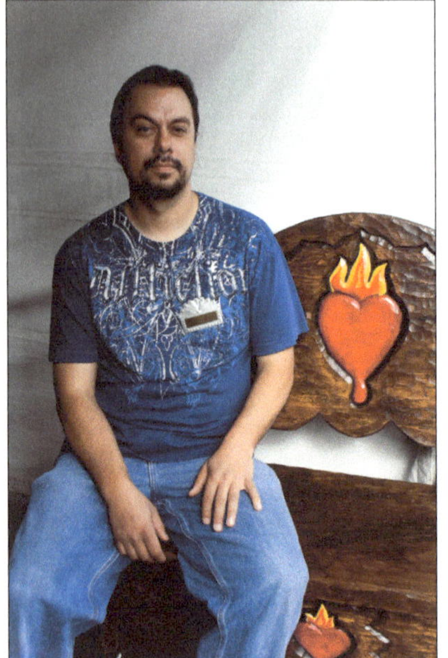

Matthew Duran

Art Form: Furniture
Contact: (505) 747-3378
Born in Fairview, New Mexico
Lives in Fairview, New Mexico
Juried into Spanish Market in 2005
Notable Awards:
Spanish Market Alan and Ann Vedder Award 2005, Second Place Furniture 2008, Third Place Furniture 2009, People's Choice Award Winter Market 2009.

Teresa May Duran

Art Form: *Retablos*
Contact: (303) 522-6994
Born in Pueblo, Colorado
Lives in Arvada, Colorado
Juried into Spanish Market in 2010
Notable Awards:
Denver Botanical Garden's Chili Harvest Poster Award 1994.
Colorado Santeros Regis University Poster Award 1997.
Chili Harvest Award 2009.
Tesoro Cultural Center Second Place Award 2010.

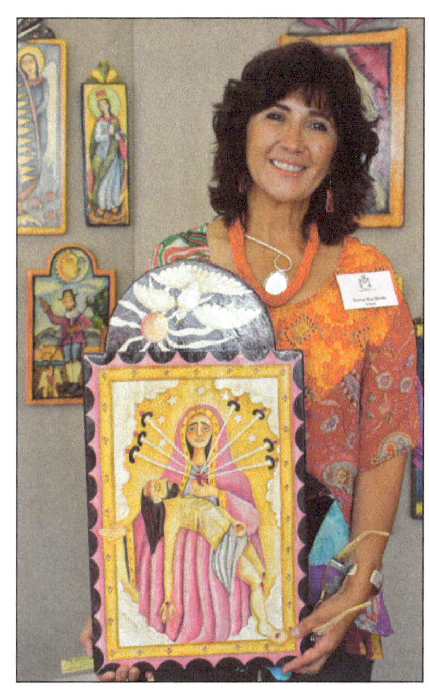

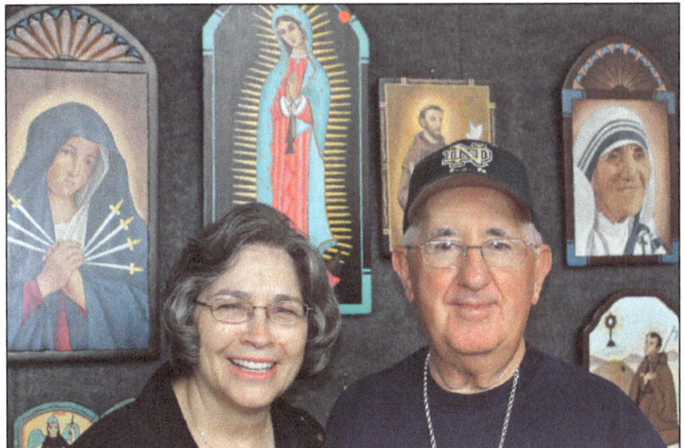

Belarmino Esquibel

Art Form: *Retablos*
Contact: (505) 471-0379
Born in Santa Fe, New Mexico
Lives in Santa Fe, New Mexico
Juried into Spanish Market in 1980
Notable Awards:

Spanish Market Honorable Mention Large *Retablos* 2001, First Place Large *Retablos* 1996 and 2002, and Master's Award for Lifetime Achievement 2010.
Feria Artistica First Place 2001 and 2003.
San Felipe de Neri Santero Market People's Choice Award 2004.

Charlie A. Esquibel

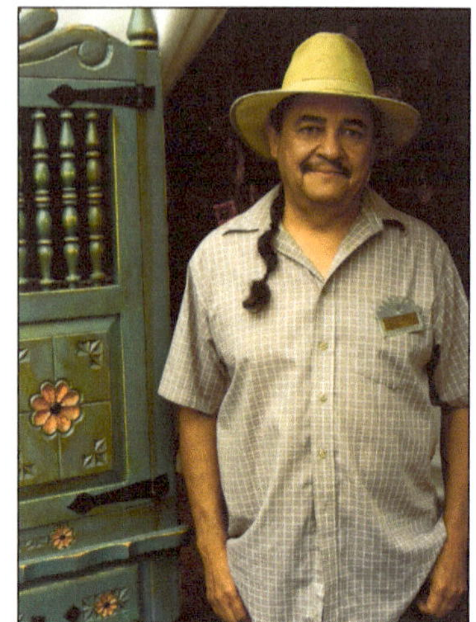

Art Form: Furniture
Contact: (505) 753-9638
Born in Española, New Mexico
Lives in Santa Cruz, New Mexico
Juried into Spanish Market in 2000
Notable Awards:
Spanish Market Second Place 2003.
Española Valley Arts Festival First Place and Best of Show 2000.

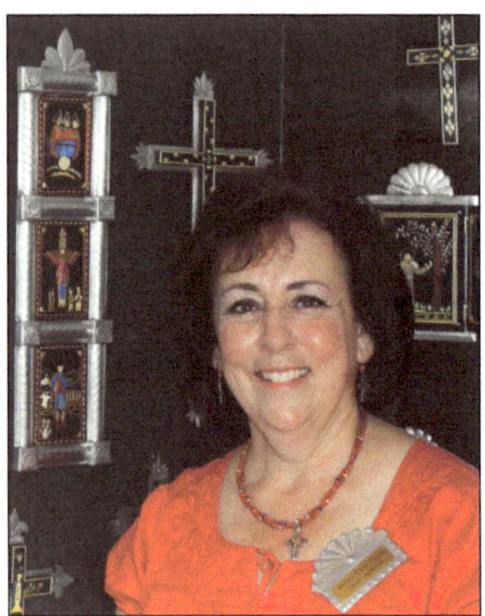

Martha Város Ewing

Art Form: Straw Appliqué
Contact: (505) 438-0009
Born in Española, New Mexico
Lives in Santa Fe, New Mexico
Juried into Spanish Market in 2004
Notable Awards:

Spanish Market First Place Diane Besser Memorial Award 2004/2005/2007, Second Place Award Diane Besser Memorial Award 2007/2009, People's Choice Award and Purchase Award and Archbishop's Award and Best of Show Award 2005, Purchase Award 2008, Florence Dibell Bartlett Award for Design 2008, First Place Mixed Media Straw Appliqué and Tinwork 2010. Her art is in the private collection of the Spanish Crown Prince and Princess and at the Vatican.

Christina Hernández Feldewert

Art Form: Tinwork
Contact: (505) 473-2952
Born in Santa Fe, New Mexico
Lives in Santa Fe, New Mexico
Juried into Spanish Market in 2005.

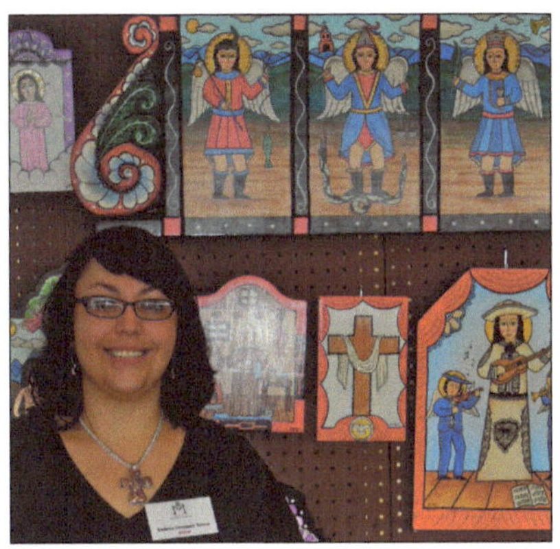

Andrea Fresquez-Baros

Art Form: *Retablos*
Contact: (505) 753-7702
Born in Española, New Mexico
Lives in Española, New Mexico
Juried into Spanish Market in 2010.

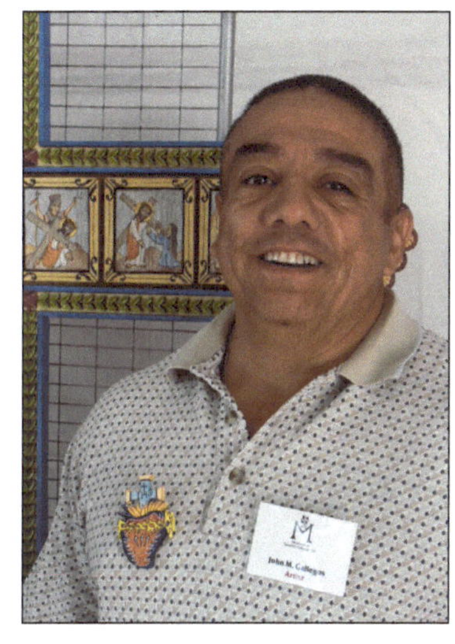

John M. Gallegos

Art Form: *Retablos*
Contact: (575) 421-1153
Born in Santa Fe, New Mexico
Lives in San José, New Mexico
Juried into Spanish Market in 1997
Notable Awards:
Spanish Market Bienvenidos Award *Retablos* 1997, First Place *Retablos* 1999 and 2010, Honorable Mention Altar Screens 2000 and 2001, Honorable Mention Award *Retablos* 2002, Third Place *Retablos* 2002, Second Place *Retablos* 2009.
St. Bernadette Art Institute Inspiration Award *Retablos* 2002.

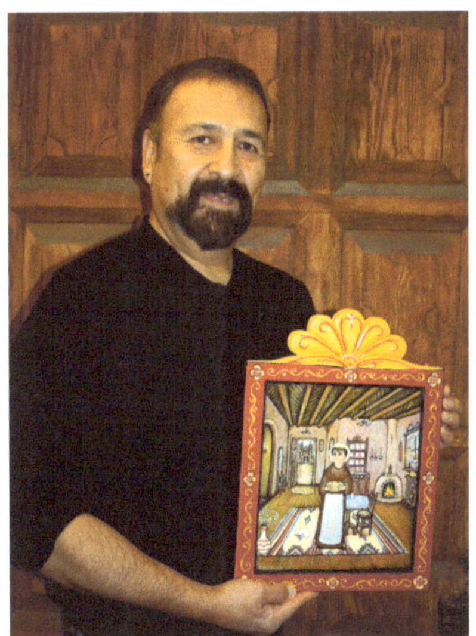

Ruben M. Gallegos

Art Form(s): Painted *Bultos*, *Retablos*, Relief Carving
Contact: (505) 463-7760
Born in Española, New Mexico
Lives in Albuquerque, New Mexico
Juried into Spanish Market in 1988
Notable Awards:

Spanish Market T-Shirt Design Selection 1996, E Boyd Award 1999, Purchase Award 2000, Honorable Mention Award Small *Retablos* 2001 and 2003, Second Place Small *Retablos* Award 2004, José Dolores López Award and Our Lady of Guadalupe Award 2008.

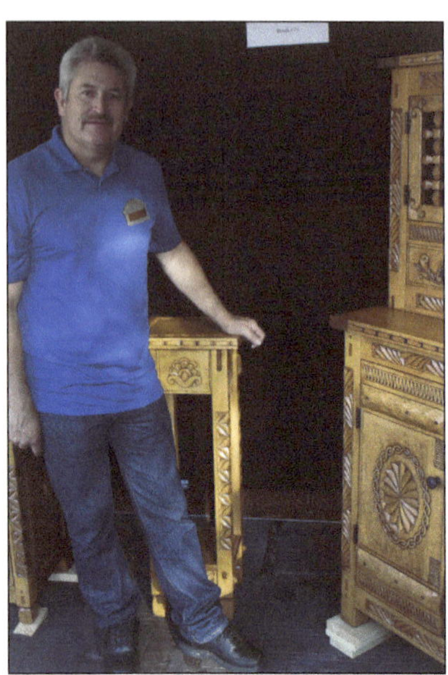

Andrew C. Garcia

Art Form: Furniture
Contact: (575) 587-2968
Born in Española, New Mexico
Lives in Peñasco, New Mexico
Juried into Spanish Market in 2004
Notable Awards:

Spanish Market Third Place Furniture 2008 and 2010, Bienvenidos Award 2004, Collaboration Award 2004 and 2008, First Place Leona Curtin Paloheimo Award for Excellence 2007/2009/2010, Best of Show and Third Place in Furniture Awards 2009.

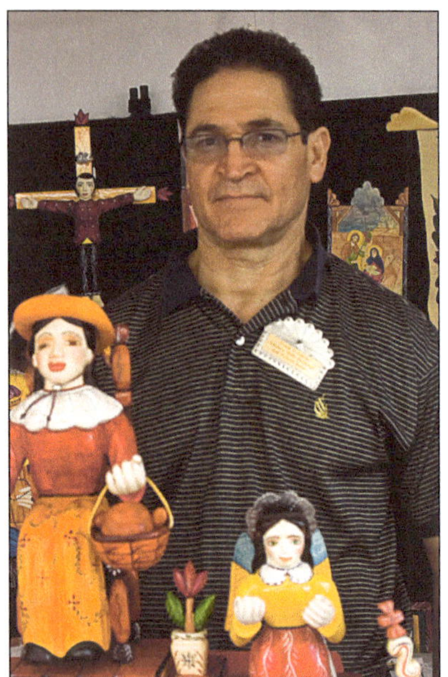

Frank L. Garcia

Art Form(s): Painted *Bultos*, *Retablos*, Hide Painting
Contact: (505) 455-3660
Born in Pojoaque, New Mexico
Lives in Santa Fe, New Mexico
Juried into Spanish Market in 1998
Notable Awards:

Spanish Market First Place Mixed Media 1999, Our Lady of Guadalupe Award Hide Painting 2006.
Tesoro Foundation First Place *Bultos* Award 2005/2007/2008/2009/2010, First Place Leather Award 2006.
New Mexico State Fair Second Place *Bultos* and Third Place Leather/ Traditional Folk Art Award 2003, Third Place *Bultos* 2004.
Española Valley Arts Festival First Place Poster Award and Second Place *Bultos* Award 2004, First Place *Bultos* Award 2003.

John Garcia

Art Form: Woodcarving
Lives in Taos, New Mexico.

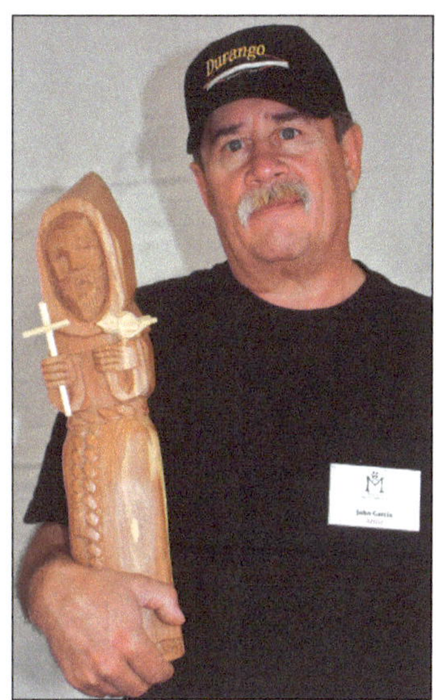

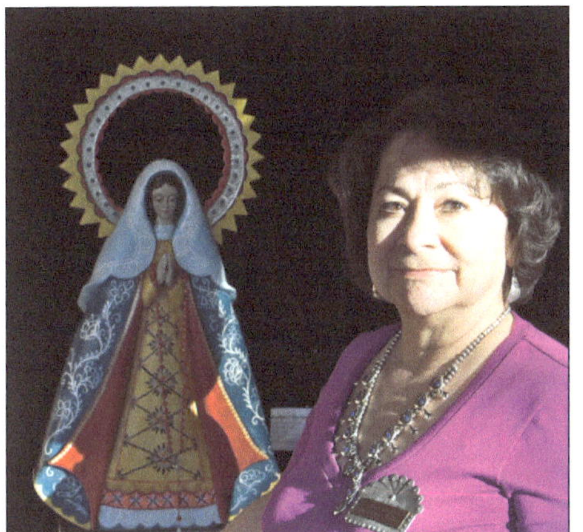

Lorrie I. Garcia

Art Form(s): Painted *Bultos*, *Retablos*
Contact: (575) 587-2968
Born in Gilman, Colorado
Lives in Peñasco, New Mexico
Juried into Spanish Market in 2001
Notable Awards:
Spanish Market Our Lady of Guadalupe 2002, Archbishop's Award 2003 and 2009, Artist Collaboration Award 2004, People's Choice Award 2003 and 2010, Alan and Ann Vedder Award 2007, Second Place Painted *Bultos* Award 2008, Second Place Large *Retablos* 2008 and 2010, Third Place Painted *Bultos* 2010.

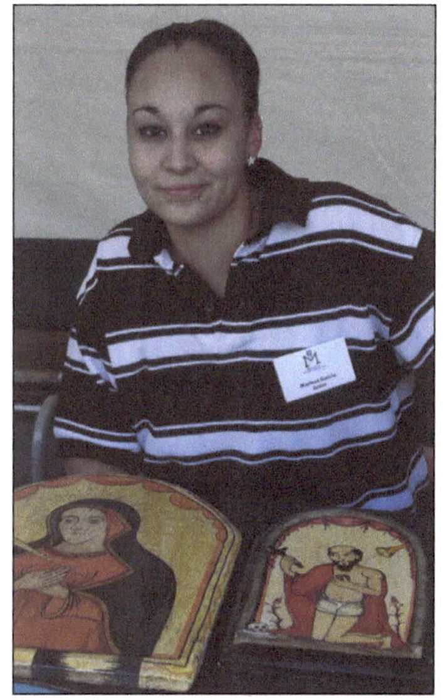

Marissa Garcia

Art Form: *Retablos*
Lives in Rio Rancho, New Mexico.

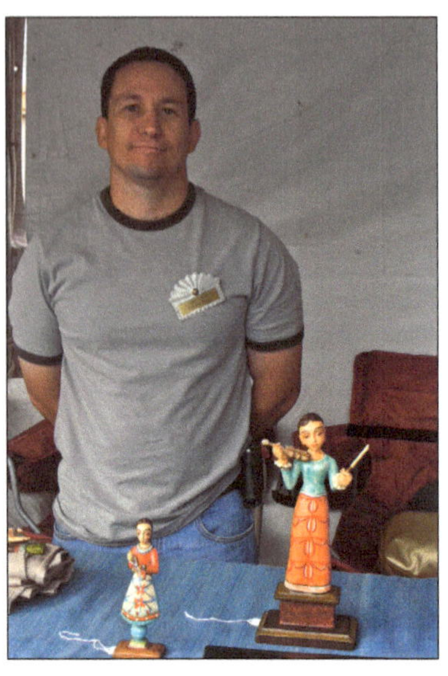

Mark A. Garcia

Art Form: Painted *Bultos*
Contact: (505) 453-0032
Born in Albuquerque, New Mexico
Lives in Albuquerque, New Mexico
Juried into Spanish Market in 2006
Notable Awards:

Spanish Market Alan and Ann Vedder Award 2007.
New Mexico State Fair Third Place Painted *Bultos* 2005, Second Place Painted *Bultos* 2006, Second Place Painted *Bultos* and Honorable Mention *Retablos* 2010.

Ronald Samuel Garcia

Art Form(s): Painted *Bultos*, *Retablos*, Relief Carving
Contact: (505) 425-3715
Born in Las Vegas, New Mexico
Lives in Mora, New Mexico
Juried into Spanish Market in 1998.

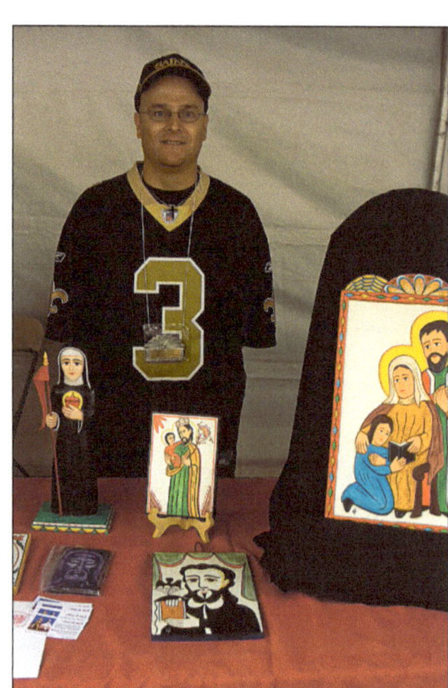

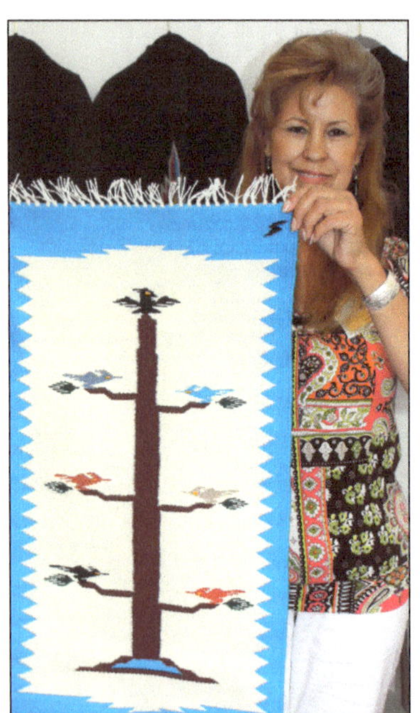

Susie G. Garcia

Art Form: Weaving
Contact: (505) 455-7574
Born in Española, New Mexico
Lives in Santa Fe, New Mexico
Juried into Spanish Market in 2008
Notable Awards:

Española Valley Arts Festival received several awards.
Pagosa Springs Fiber Art Show First Place Woven Purse.
Taos Wool Festival Third Place.

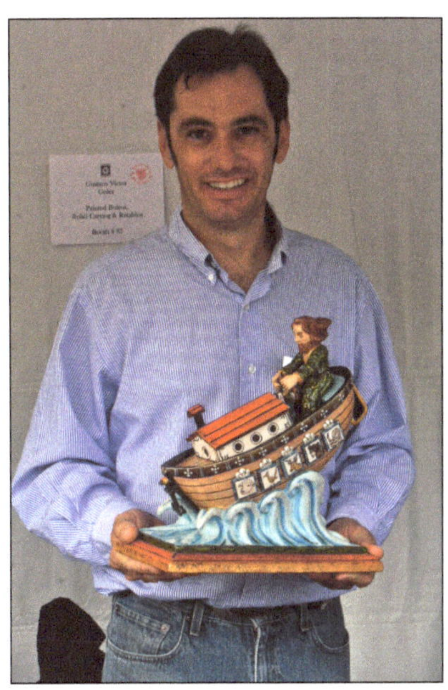

Gustavo Victor Goler

Art Form(s): Painted *Bultos*, *Retablos*, Relief Carving
Contact: (575) 758-9538
Born in Buenos Aires, Argentina
Lives in Talpa, New Mexico
Juried into Spanish Market in 1988
Notable Awards:

Spanish Market Grand Prize Best of Show Awards 1992 and 1994, First Place in *Bultos* en Nicho and People's Choice Award 2000, First Place *Bultos* en Nicho and E Boyd Award 2002, First Place *Bultos* en Nicho and Second Place *Bultos* 2003, First Place *Bultos* and Archbishop's Award 2004, First Place *Bultos* and Purchase Award 2005, Second Place *Bultos* 2006, Honorable Mention 2007, First Place Award and Purchase Award 2008, First Place Altar Screen and Design Award. Taos Invites Taos First Place Santos and Second Place Best of Show 2000.

Julia R. Gómez

Art Form: Colcha Embroidery
Contact: (505) 471-4626
Born in Madrid, New Mexico
Lives in Santa Fe, New Mexico
Juried into Spanish Market in 2002
Notable Awards:

Spanish Market First Place 2002 and 2003, Second Place 2003, Purchase Award 2009, Grand Prize for Best of Show 2010. New Mexico State Fair Santos of New Mexico Award 2005.

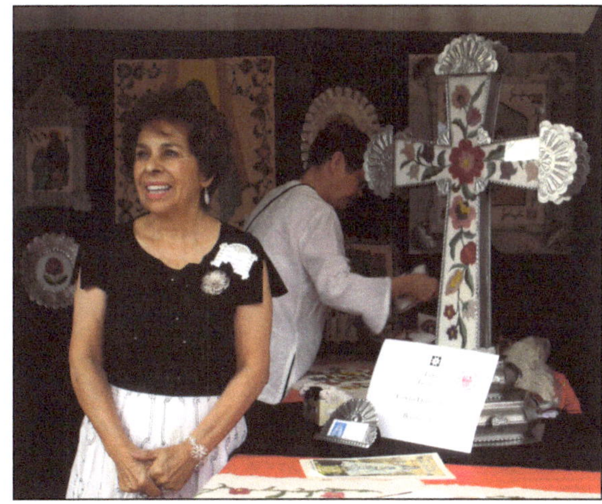

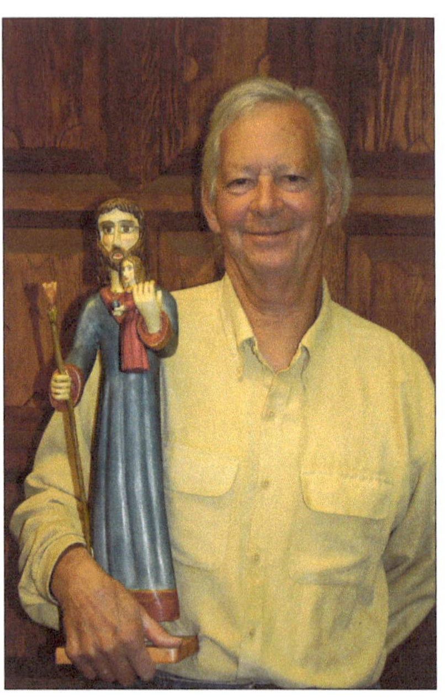

Andrew A. Gonzales

Art Form: Painted *Bultos*
Contact: (505) 699-3875
Born in Santa Fe, New Mexico
Lives in Los Ojos, New Mexico
Juried into Spanish Market in 1994
Notable Awards:
Spanish Market Boeckman Award 1997, Design Award 2002.

María Fernández Graves

Art Form: Colcha Embroidery
Lives in Ranchos de Taos, New Mexico.

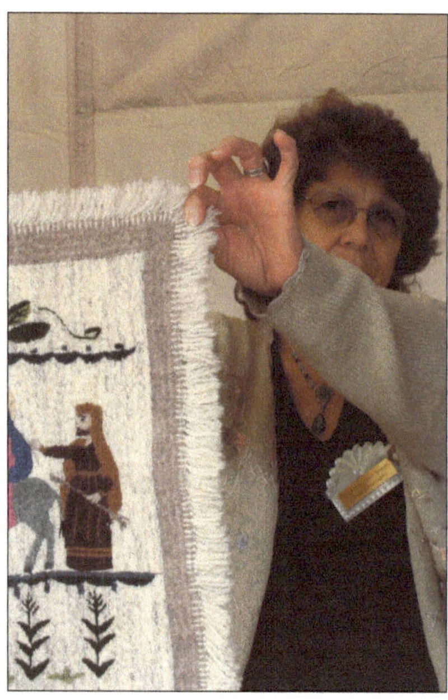

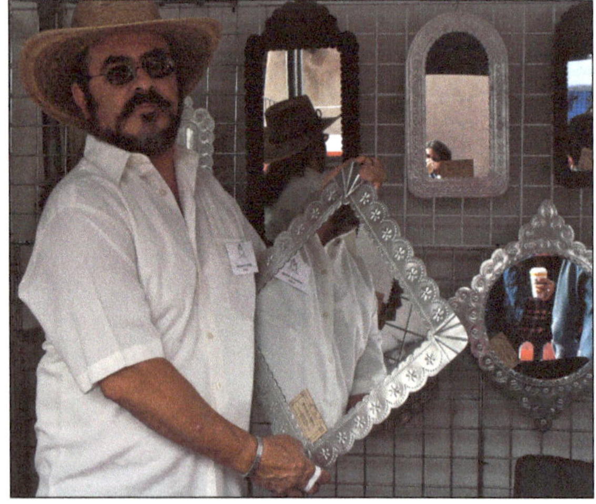

Michael E. Griego

Art Form: Tinwork
Contact: (505) 471-3017
Born in Oakland, California
Lives in Santa Fe, New Mexico
Juried into Spanish Market in 1988
Notable Awards:
Spanish Market First Place 2005.
New Mexico State Fair and El Rancho de las Golondrinas Award numerous times.

Rob Guillen

Art Form: Relief Carving
Lives in Colorado Springs, Colorado.

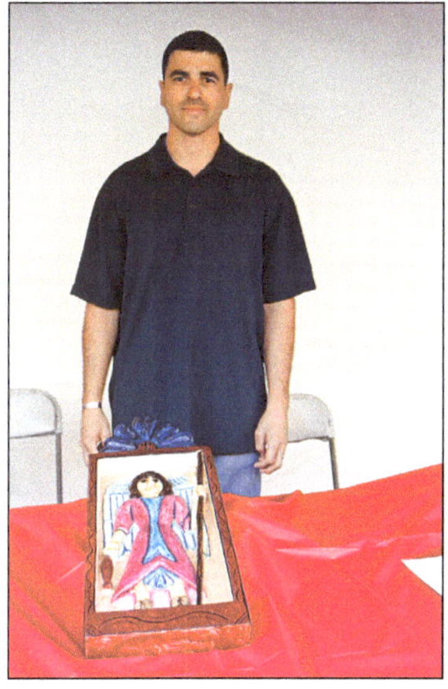

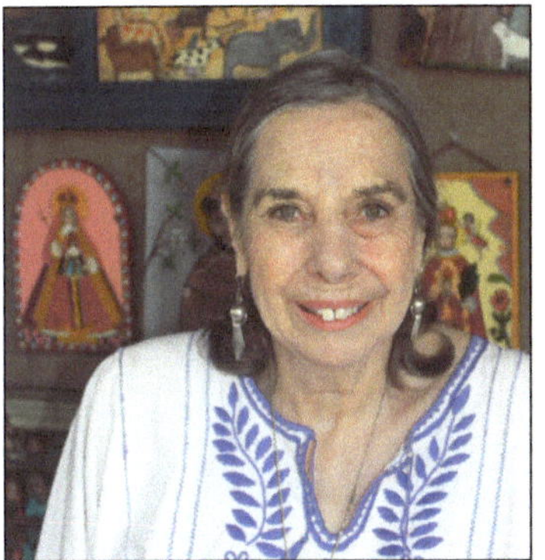

Mónica Sosaya Halford

Art Form(s): Colcha Embroidery, Altar Screens, *Retablos*
Contact: (505) 982-4175
Born in Santa Fe, New Mexico
Lives in Santa Fe, New Mexico
Juried into Spanish Market in 1979
Notable Awards:
Spanish Market awards in 1979/1980/1981/1982/ 1984/1985/1987/ 1988/2000, Master's Award for Lifetime Achievement 1994.
Santa Fe Mayor's Award for Traditional Art 2000.
New Mexico Governor's Award 2001.

Rita Padilla Haufmann

Art Form: Weaving
Contact: (505) 310-2399
Born in Santa Fe, New Mexico
Lives in Tesuque, New Mexico
Juried into Spanish Market in 1989
Notable Awards:
Spanish Market First and Second Place Awards, Jake Trujillo Award for Excellence in Weaving, Purchase Award, La Lana Award for Innovative Use of Color.
Museum of Indian Arts and Culture First and Second Place Awards.
Taylor Museum First Place and Purchase Award.

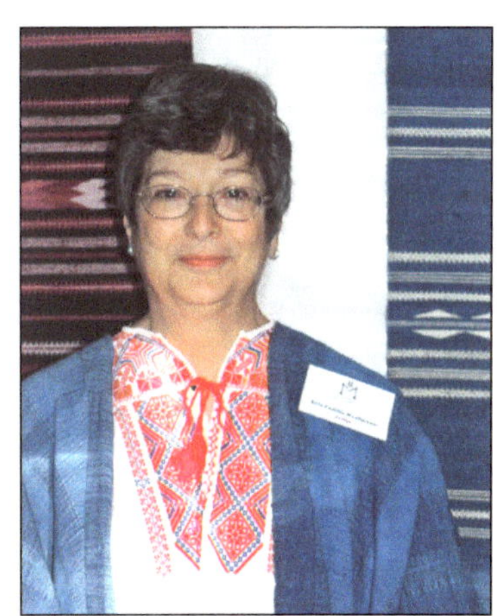

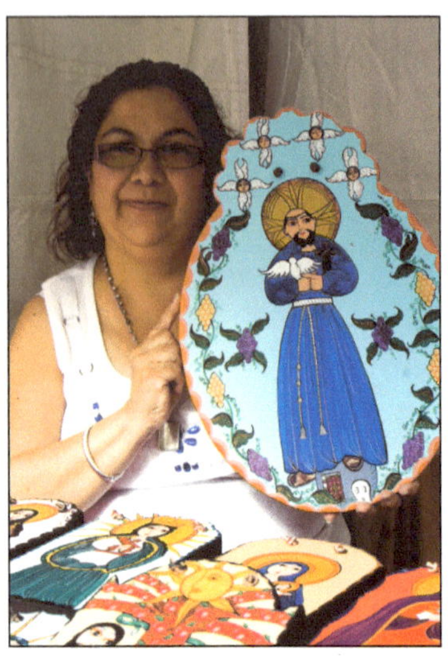

Elena Miera Herrera
Art Form: *Retablos*
Lives in Rio Rancho, New Mexico.

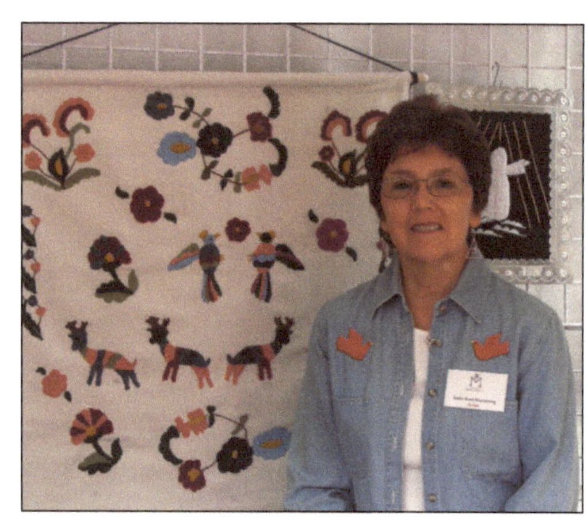

Anita Rael Hisenberg
Art Form: Colcha Embroidery
Contact: (505) 471-3017
Born in Santa Fe, New Mexico
Lives in Santa Fe, New Mexico
Juried into Spanish Market in 2005
Notable Awards:
Spanish Market Second Place 2005.
New Mexico State Fair First Place.

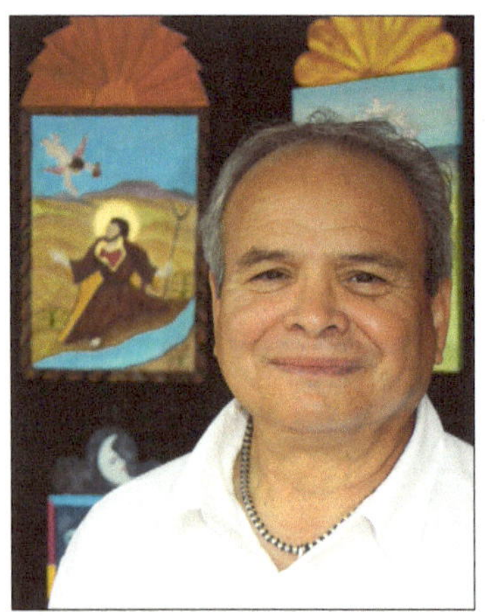

John Jiménez
Art Form: *Retablos*
Contact: (505) 982-1418
Born in Clayton, New Mexico
Lives in Tesuque, New Mexico
Juried into Spanish Market in 1974
Notable Awards:

Spanish Market First Place *Retablos* 1978/1979/1981/2002/2003,
Second Place 1979 and 1983, Third Place 1979,
Master's Award for Lifetime Achievement 2004.
Mayor's Recognition Award for Arts in Education 1988.

Cecilia Leitner

Art Form: *Retablos*
Contact: (505) 920-5145
Born in Santa Fe, New Mexico
Lives in Chimayo, New Mexico
Juried into Spanish Market in 2010.

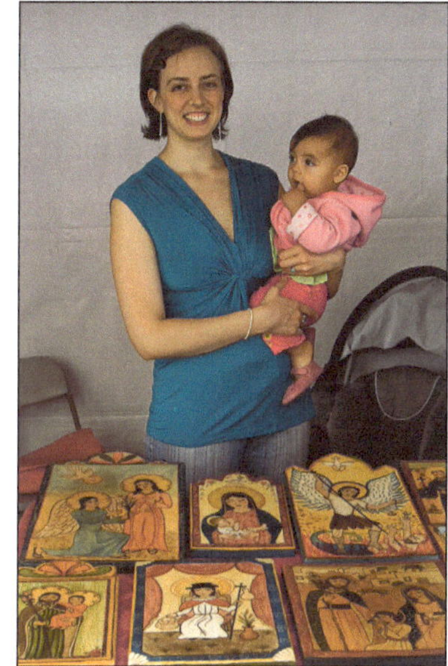

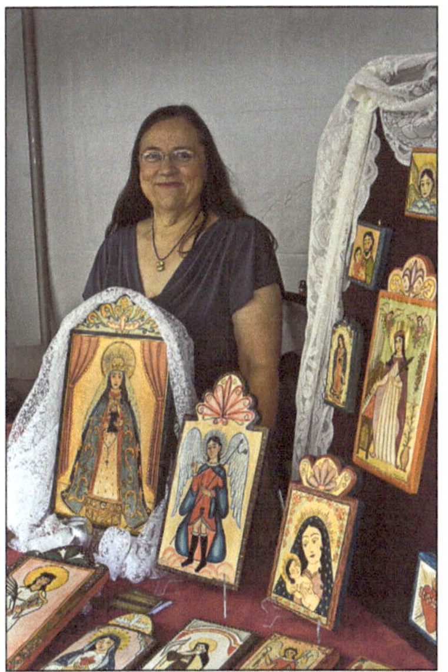

Ellen Chávez de Leitner

Art Form: *Retablos*
Contact: (505) 920-9728
Born in Embudo, New Mexico
Lives in Chimayo, New Mexico
Juried into Spanish Market in 1988
Notable Awards:

Spanish Market Bienvenidos Award, 1988, Collaboration Award with silversmith Luis Mojica 2000, Purchase Award 2002.

Española Valley Arts and Crafts Festival Best of Category Award 1990.

New Mexico State Fair Third Place 1995.

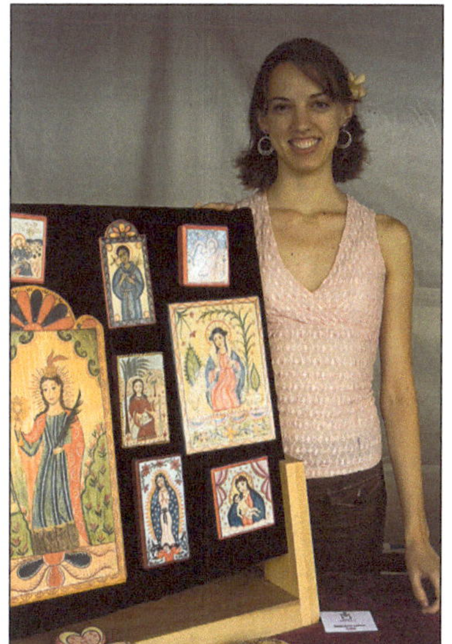

Genevieve Leitner

Art Form: *Retablos*
Contact: (505) 501-8092
Born in Chimayo, New Mexico
Lives in Chimayo, New Mexico
Juried into Spanish Market in 2005.

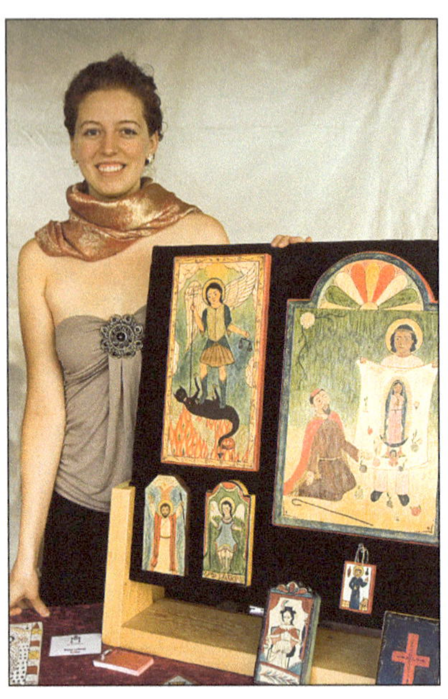

Rose Leitner
Art Form: *Retablos*
Contact: (505) 310-5220
Born in Chimayo, New Mexico
Lives in Chimayo, New Mexico
Juried into Spanish Market in 2008.

Patrick Leyba
Art Form: Furniture
Contact: (505) 471-8894
Born in Embudo, New Mexico
Lives in Santa Fe, New Mexico
Juried into Spanish Market in 2009.

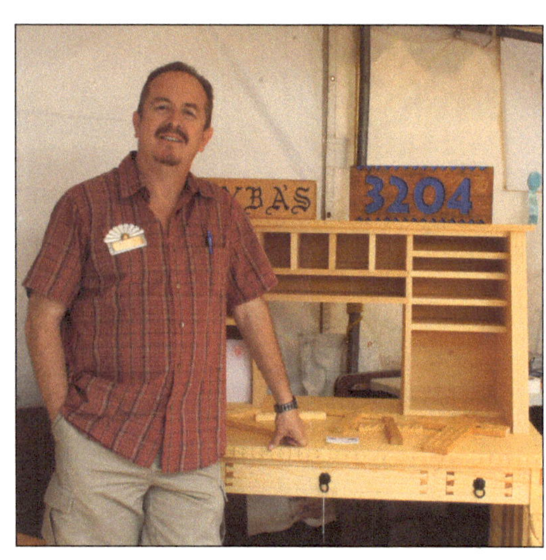

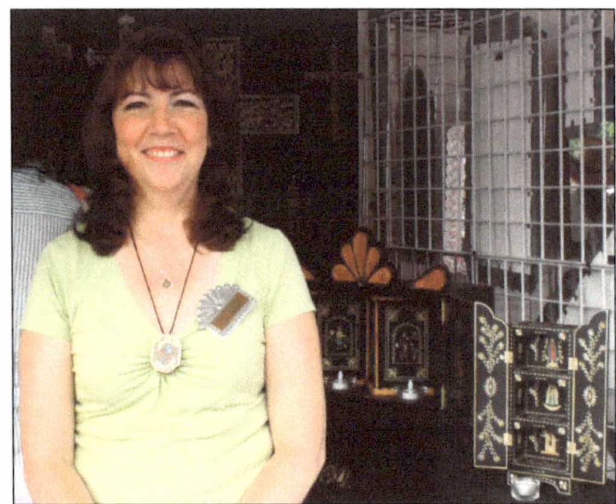

Judy Vároz Long
Art Form: Straw Appliqué
Contact: (505) 471-0863
Born in Los Alamos, New Mexico
Lives in Santa Fe, New Mexico
Juried into Spanish Market in 2005
Notable Awards:
Spanish Market Honorable Mention Diane Besser Memorial Award 2005, Archbishop's Award 2006

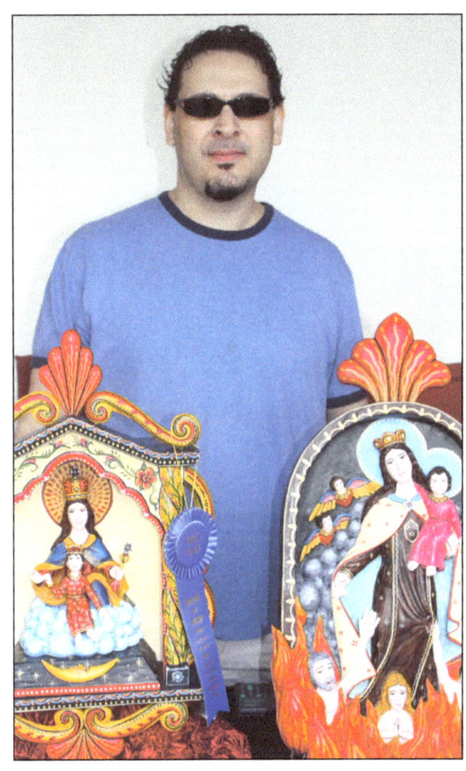

Arthur López

Art Form(s): Painted *Bultos*, Relief Carving
Contact: (505) 986-9540
Born in Santa Fe, New Mexico
Lives in Santa Fe, New Mexico
Juried into Spanish Market in 2000
Notable Awards:

Spanish Market Alan and Ann Vedder and Second Place *Bultos* en Nicho 2001, Florence Dibell Bartlett Award 2002, Directors' Award, Second Place Painted *Bultos* and Poster Award 2004, Artist Collaboration Award with wife Bernadette 2005, Purchase Award, Second Place *Bultos* en Nicho, and Honorable Mention Painted *Bultos* 2006, Boeckman Award for New Directions and Second Place Altar Screen 2007, Wood Relief Award 2008, Collaboration Award with wife Bernadette and First Place *Bultos* en Nicho, Florence Dibell Bartlett Award 2009, First Place *Bultos* en Nicho 2010.

New Mexico State Fair Third Place *Bultos* 2000.

New Mexico Secretary of State Recognition for Enhancing Quality of Life.

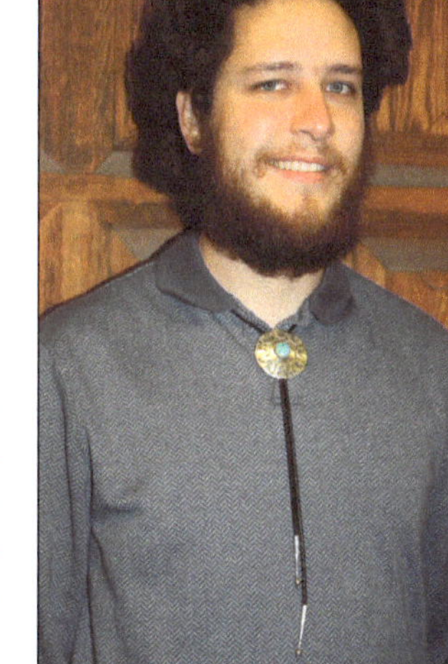

Bo López

Art Form: Precious Metals
Contact: (505) 995-1175
Born in Santa Fe, New Mexico
Lives in Santa Fe, New Mexico
Juried into Spanish Market in 2001.

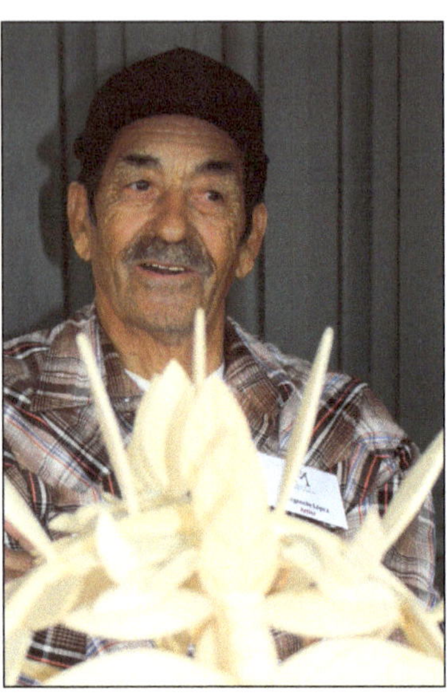

Eurgencio López

Art Form: Woodcarving
Contact: (505) 351-4820
Born in Córdova, New Mexico
Lives in Córdova, New Mexico
Juried into Spanish Market in 1997
Notable Awards:

Spanish Market Third Place 1997.
Feria Artistica Second Place 2002.
New Mexico State Fair Best of Show 1984.

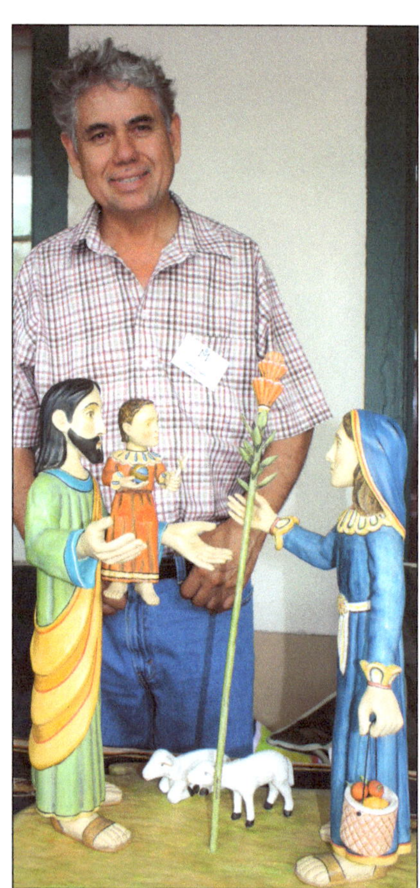

Felix A. López

Art Form(s): Painted *Bultos*, Straw Appliqué
Contact: (505) 753-2785
Born in Gilman, Colorado
Lives in Española, New Mexico
Juried into Spanish Market in 1976
Notable Awards:

Spanish Market First Place multiple times in Painted *Bultos*, First Place in Painted *Bultos* en Nicho, First Place Straw Appliqué, Purchase Award, Florence Dibell Bartlett Award, E Boyd Award, People's Choice Award, Archbishop's Award, Grand Prize for Best in Show 1998, Master's Award for Lifetime Achievement 2007.
National Endowment for the Arts Visual Artist Fellowship.

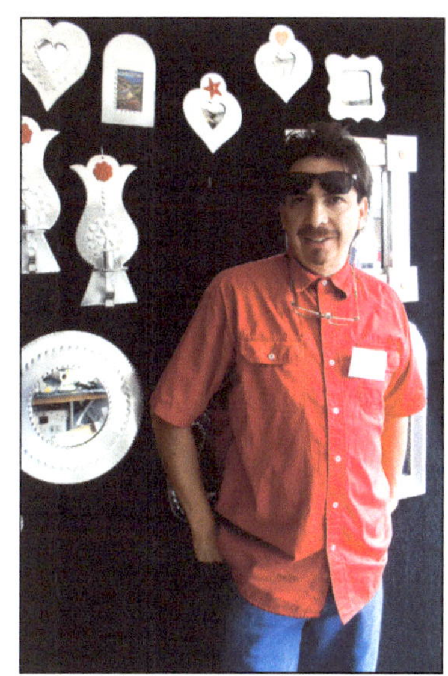

Fred Ray López
Art Form: Tinwork
Contact: (505) 473-0261
Born in Henderson, Nevada
Lives in Santa Fe, New Mexico
Juried into Spanish Market in 1992
Notable Awards:
Spanish Market First Place Precious Metals 1992 and 1993,
First Place Tinwork 1994.
Phoenix Home & Garden Show Masters of the Southwest Award.
Selected to create the New Mexico State Department of Tourism Logo 1997.

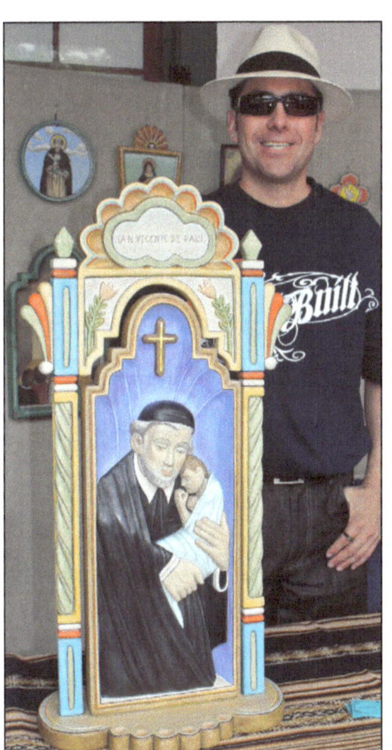

Joseph A. López
Art Form: Painted *Bultos*
Contact: (505) 753-2785
Born in Orange, California
Lives in Española, New Mexico
Juried into Spanish Market in 1978
Notable Awards:
Spanish Market First Place *Bultos*, First Place Our Lady of Guadalupe Award, First Place Painted Wood Relief, E Boyd Award, Alan and Ann Vedder Award, Purchase Award, Florence Dibell Bartlett Award.

Juan López
Art Form: Precious Metals
Contact: (505) 980-7575
Born in Corrales, New Mexico
Lives in Corrales, New Mexico
Juried into Spanish Market in 1999
Notable Awards:
Director's Award for Spanish Market Poster 2010.

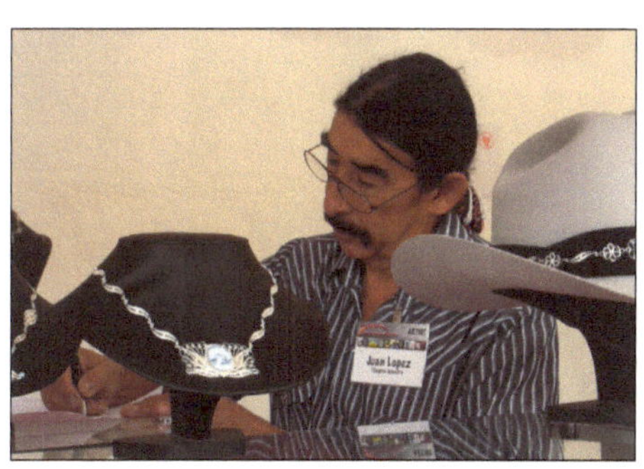

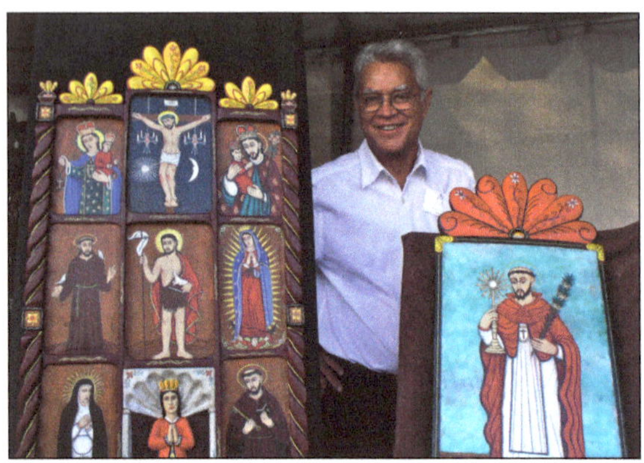

Peter E. López

Art Form(s): Painted *Bultos*, *Retablos*, Relief Carving
Contact: (505) 425-8214
Born in Las Vegas, New Mexico
Lives in Montezuma, New Mexico
Juried into Spanish Market in 1990
Notable Awards:

Spanish Market Poster Award 1993, Best Gesso and Wood Relief Carving 1999, Second Place Painted *Bultos* 2002, Second Place Large *Retablos* 2001 and 2005, Second Place Large *Retablos* 2006.

New Mexico Secretary of State Recognition for Enhancing Quality of Life 2000.

New Mexico State Fair Purchase Award, *Bultos* and Third Place Award *Retablos* 2008.

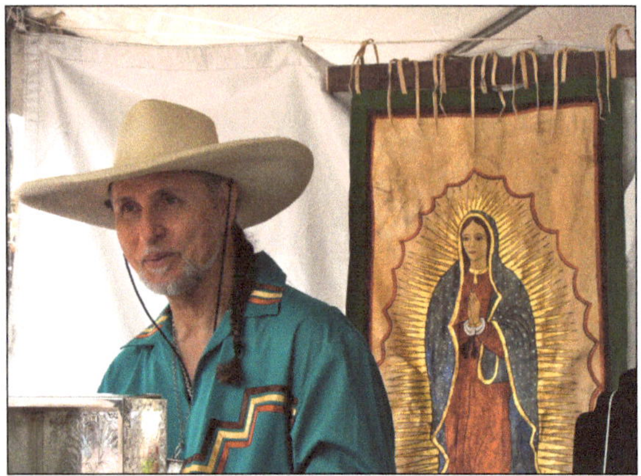

Ramón José López

Art Form(s): *Bultos*, Furniture, *Retablos*, Precious Metal, Hide Painting
Contact: (505) 988-4976
Born in Santa Fe, New Mexico
Lives in Santa Fe, New Mexico
Juried into Spanish Market in 1981
Notable Awards:

Spanish Market Grand Prize for Best in Show 1983/1985/1989/1993, First Place Awards1981/1982/ 1983/1984/1990/1992/1993/1994/1995/1996/1997, six Second Prizes and three Special Awards, Masters Award for Lifetime Achievement, 2008.

National Endowment for the Arts National Heritage Fellowship Award as Master Artist 1997.

Art in New Mexico State Capital and Smithsonian Institution Collections.

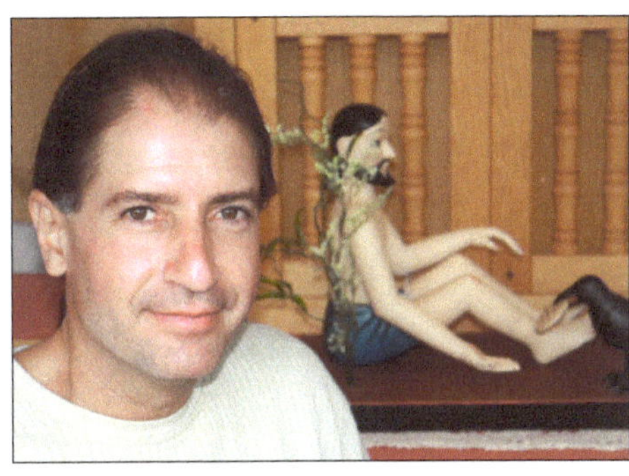

Raymond López
Art Form(s): Painted *Bultos*, Furniture, *Retablos*
Contact: (505) 920-5946
Born in Santa Fe, New Mexico
Lives in Pojoaque, New Mexico
Juried into Spanish Market in 1992
Notable Awards:
Spanish Market First Place Furniture 1994, Poster Award and First Place Mixed Media 1995, Alan and Ann Vedder Award 1996, First Place Painted *Bultos* 1997.

Rosina López de Short
Art Form(s): Relief Carving, *Retablos*
Contact: (830) 768-1734
Born in Santa Fe, New Mexico
Lives in Del Rio, Texas
Juried into Spanish Market in 1987.

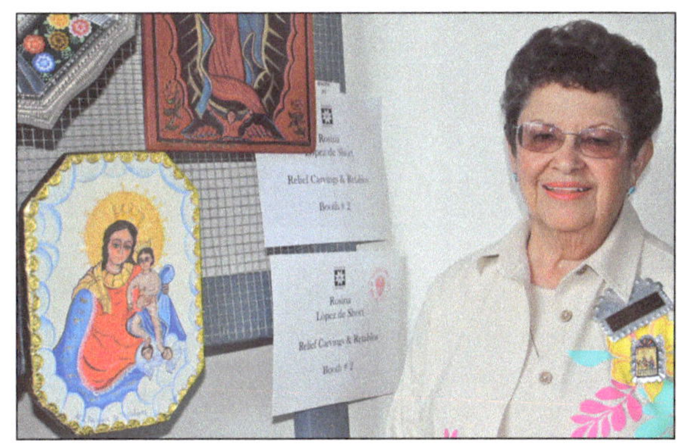

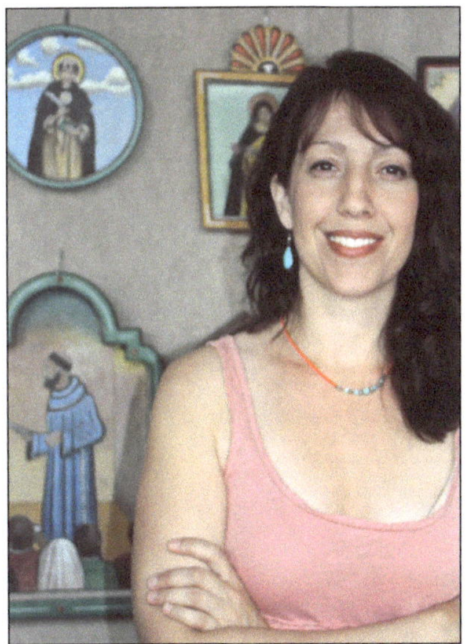

Krissa López-Moya
Art Form(s): *Retablos*, Straw Appliqué
Contact: (505) 753-2785
Born in Santa Fe, New Mexico
Lives in Española, New Mexico
Juried into Spanish Market in 1978
Notable Awards:
Spanish Market First Place and Second Place Straw Appliqué, Florence Dibell Bartlett Award *Retablos*.

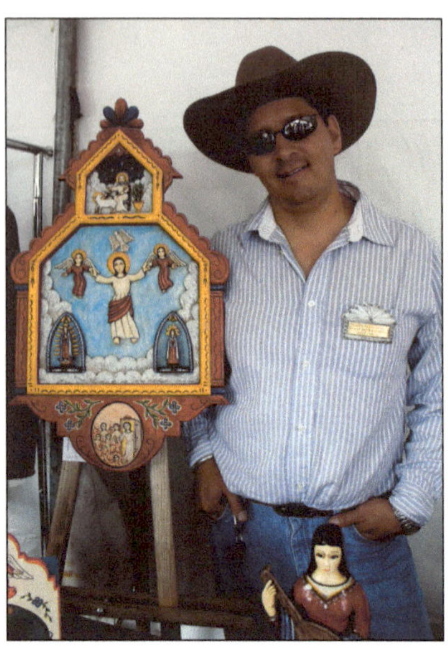

Frankie Nazario Lucero

Art Form(s): *Retablos, Bultos*, Relief Carving
Contact: (505) 820-2149
Born in Santa Fe, New Mexico
Lives in Santa Fe, New Mexico
Juried into Spanish Market in 1995
Notable Awards:

Spanish Market Poster Award 2009, First Place Collaboration and Purchase Award for *Bultos*/Iron.
New Mexico State Fair Best of Show.
Santa Fe County Fair Best of Show.

Gregory D. Lucero

Art Form: Tinwork
Contact: (505) 670-2289
Born in Santa Fe, New Mexico
Lives in Santa Fe, New Mexico
Juried into Spanish Market in 2010
Notable Awards:

Spanish Market Bienvenidos Award 2010.
New Mexico State Fair First Place Tinwork.
New Mexico Veterans Art Show First Place 2009, Second Place 2010.
National Veterans Creative Art Fest Silver Medal 2010.
Northern New Mexico College First Place 2010.

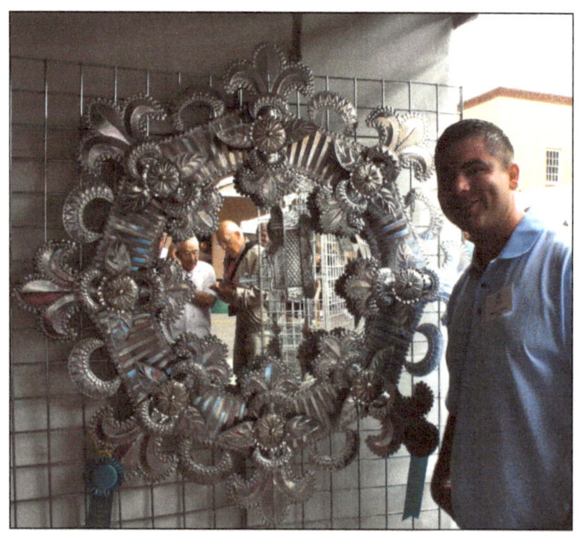

José A. Lucero

Art Form(s): Painted *Bultos*, *Retablos*
Contact: (505) 231-9155
Born in Santa Fe, New Mexico
Lives in Santa Fe, New Mexico
Juried into Spanish Market in 1997
Notable Awards:
Spanish Market Purchase Award, First Place Altar Screen, Hispanic Heritage Award 1999, Second Place Small *Retablos* 2002, Honorable Mention Small *Retablos* 2006.

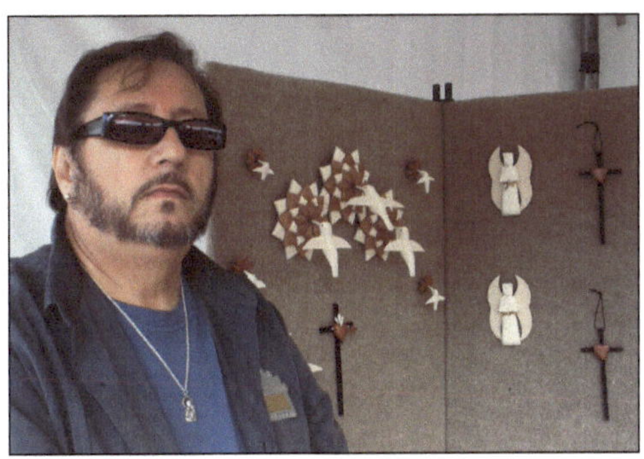

José Floyd Lucero

Art Form: Woodcarving
Contact: (505) 471-0575
Born in Santa Fe, New Mexico
Lives in Santa Fe, New Mexico
Juried into Spanish Market in 1988
Notable Awards:
Spanish Market Second Place Unpainted *Bultos* 1999 and 2000, First Place Unpainted *Bultos* 1996, Creativity Award and Purchase Award 2000, José Dolores López Memorial Award 2001 and 2006, Second Place Mixed Media Award 2002, Woodcarving Award 2008. *Feria Artistica* First Place 2001.

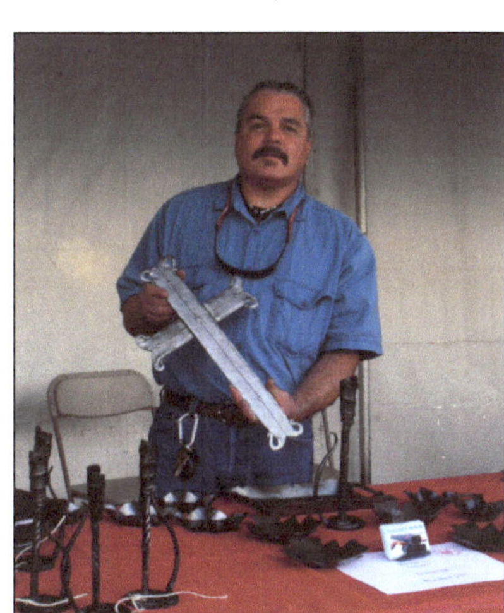

Steven A. Lucero

Art Form: Ironwork
Contact: (505) 470-3858
Born in Santa Fe, New Mexico
Lives in Santa Fe, New Mexico
Juried into Spanish Market in 2009
Notable Awards:
Spanish Market Hispanic Heritage Award 1999, Second Place Revival Arts Award 2001, Honorable Mention Revival Arts 2004; Purchase, Utilitarian and Collaboration Award 2007.

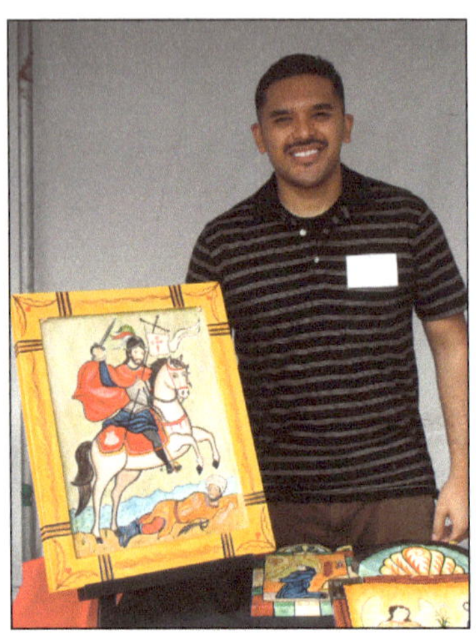

Tim Lucero

Art Form: *Retablos*
Contact: (505) 459-8112
Born in Albuquerque, New Mexico
Lives in Rio Rancho, New Mexico
Juried into Spanish Market in 2009
Notable Awards:
Spanish Market Third Place Small *Retablos* 2010.

Verne L. Lucero

Art Form: Tinwork
Contact: (505) 896-2221
Born in Albuquerque, New Mexico
Lives in Rio Rancho, New Mexico
Juried into Spanish Market in 1997
Notable Awards:
Spanish Market Bienvenidos Award 1997.
Española Valley Arts Festival People's Choice, Best of Show.
National Veterans Creative Art Gold Medal 2006,
Silver Medal 2008,
Bronze Medal and Vietnam Award 2009.
Governor's Award for Lifetime
Achievement in the Arts 2007.

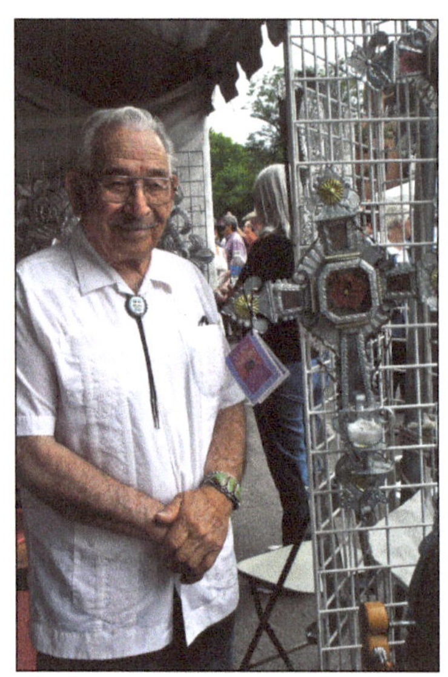

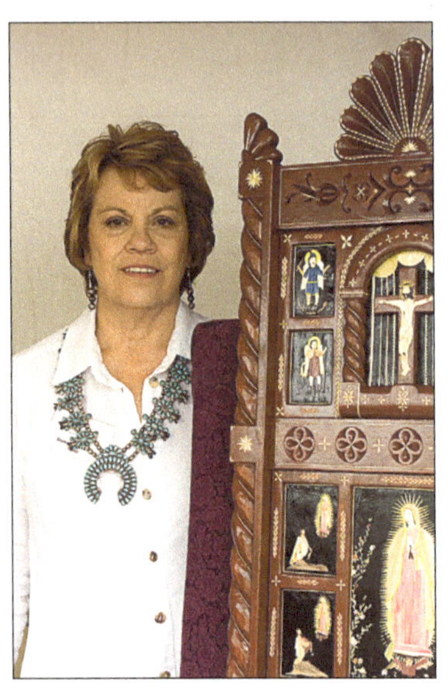

Diana Moya Lujan

Art Form: Straw Appliqué
Contact: (505) 983-5410
Born in Santa Fe, New Mexico
Lives in Santa Fe, New Mexico
Juried into Spanish Market in 1996
Notable Awards:
Spanish Market Second Place Bulto en Nicho and Utilitarian Award 2002,
Second Place Straw Appliqué 2004 and 2005, Purchase Award 2004,
Honorable Mention Mixed Media 2005, First Place Straw Appliqué 2008.

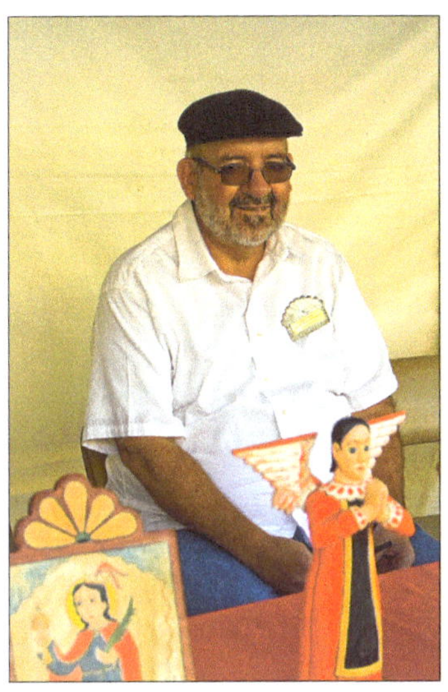

Ernie R. Lujan

Art Form(s): Painted *Bultos*, *Retablos*, Relief Carving
Contact: (505) 455-7417
Born in Santa Fe, New Mexico
Lives in Nambe, New Mexico
Juried into Spanish Market in 1991
Notable Awards:

Spanish Market Hispanic Heritage Award 1991 and 1993.
New Mexico State Fair First Place Painted *Bultos* 1993.

Jerome P. Lujan

Art Form(s): Painted *Bultos*, *Retablos*
Contact: (505) 455-1123
Born in Santa Fe, New Mexico
Lives in Nambe, New Mexico
Juried into Spanish Market in 1991
Notable Awards:
Spanish Market Purchase Award 1998 and 2004,
Second Place Painted *Bultos* 1999 and 2001,
Second Place Mixed Media 2000,
New Directions Award 2001, Third Place Painted *Bultos* and
Third Place Bulto en Nicho 2002,
Collaboration Award and Third Place Bulto en Nicho 2003,
E Boyd Award and Third Place Painted *Bultos* Award 2005,
Gesso Relief Award 2010.

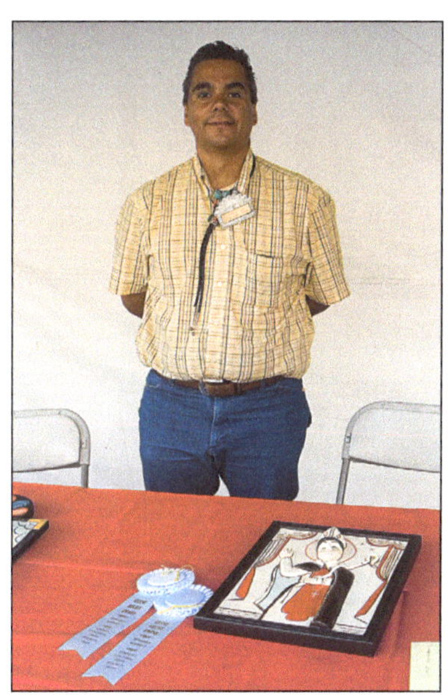

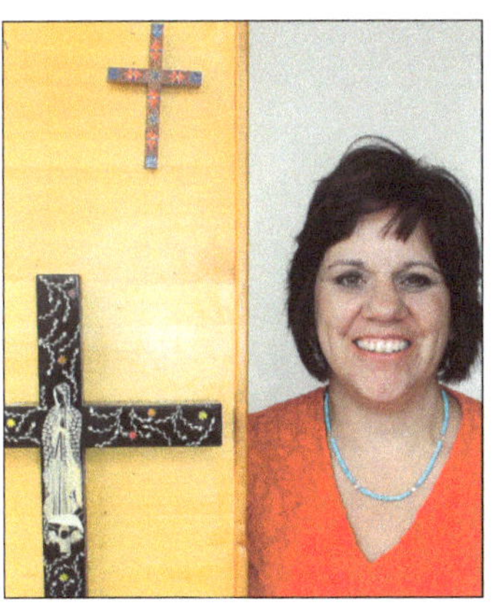

Lenise Lujan-Mártinez

Art Form: Straw Appliqué
Contact: (505) 820-6127
Born in Santa Fe, New Mexico
Lives in Santa Fe, New Mexico
Juried into Spanish Market in 2000
Notable Awards:

Spanish Market Purchase Award, Second Place Straw Appliqué, and Florence Dibell Bartlett Award 2001.
Susan Black Foundation Honorable Mention 2010.
New Mexico State Fair First Place Straw Appliqué 2008.

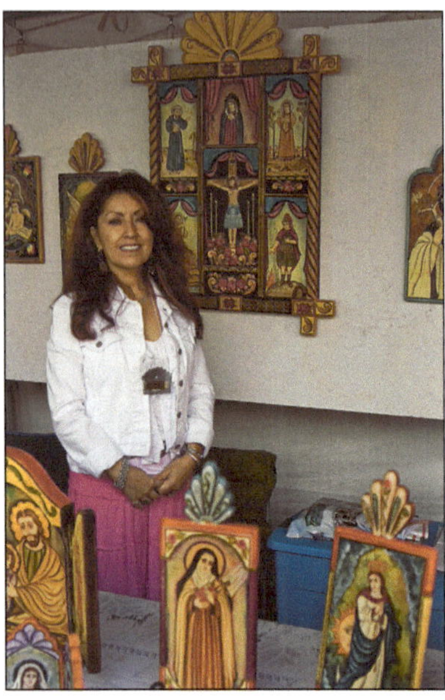

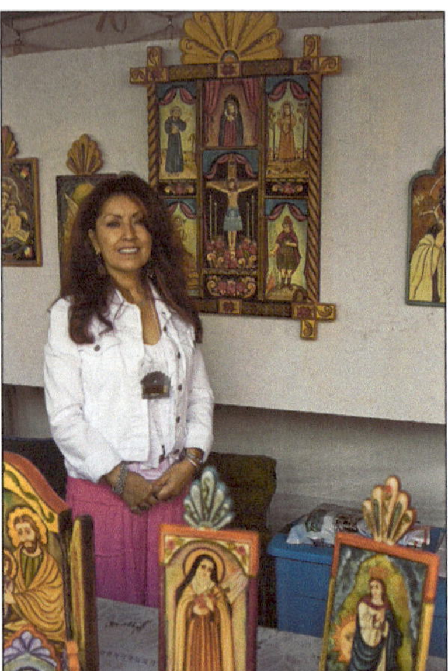

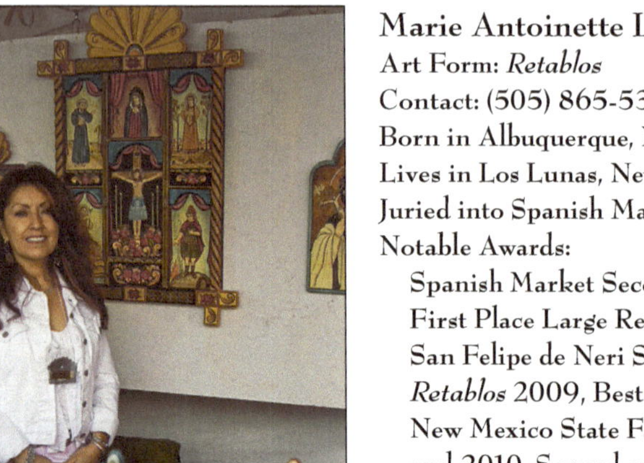

Marie Antoinette Luna

Art Form: *Retablos*
Contact: (505) 865-5302
Born in Albuquerque, New Mexico
Lives in Los Lunas, New Mexico
Juried into Spanish Market in 2003
Notable Awards:

Spanish Market Second Place Altar Screen 2006, First Place Large Retablo 2007.
San Felipe de Neri Santero Market First Place *Retablos* 2009, Best of Show *Retablos* 2010.
New Mexico State Fair First Place *Retablos* 2009 and 2010, Second and Third Place *Retablos* 2010.

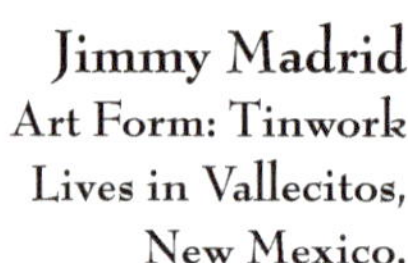

Jimmy Madrid

Art Form: Tinwork
Lives in Vallecitos, New Mexico.

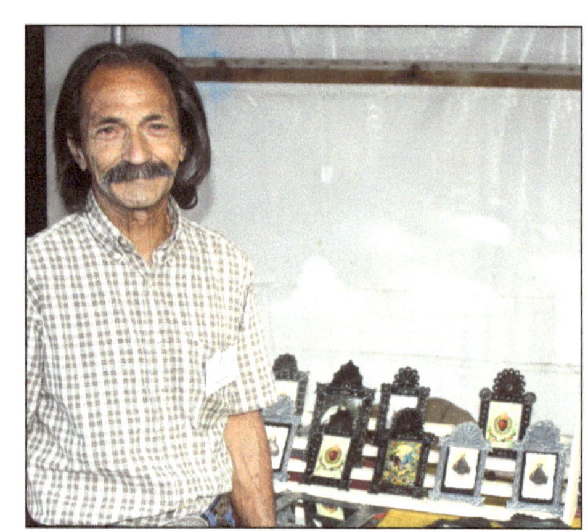

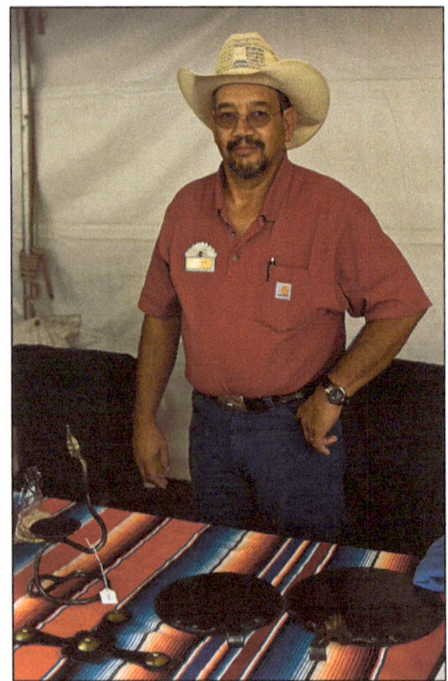

Larry E. Madrid

Art Form: Ironwork
Contact: (505) 865-2858
Born in Belen, New Mexico
Lives in Los Lunas, New Mexico
Juried into Spanish Market in 2008
Notable Awards:

Spanish Market Utilitarian Award 2008, Ironwork Award 2009.

Nicolas Madrid
Art Form: Tinwork
Lives in Santa Cruz, New Mexico.

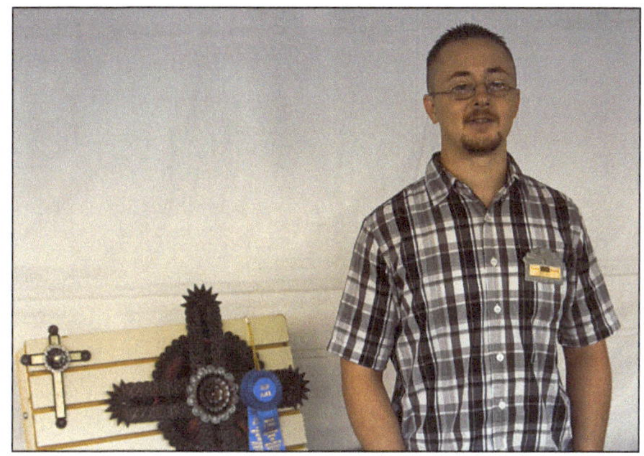

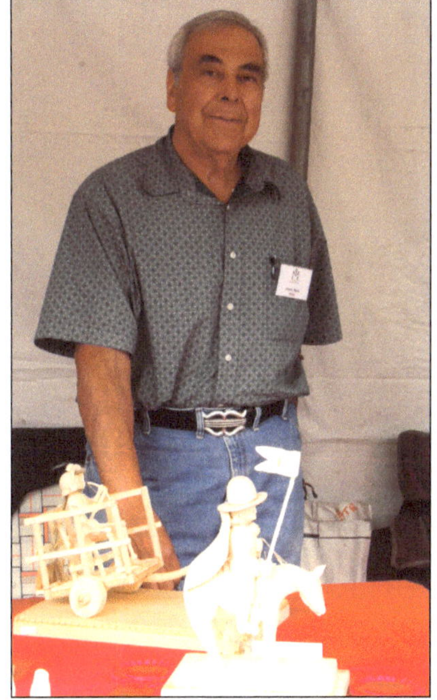

José U. Maes
Art Form: Woodcarving
Lives in San Juan Pueblo, New Mexico.

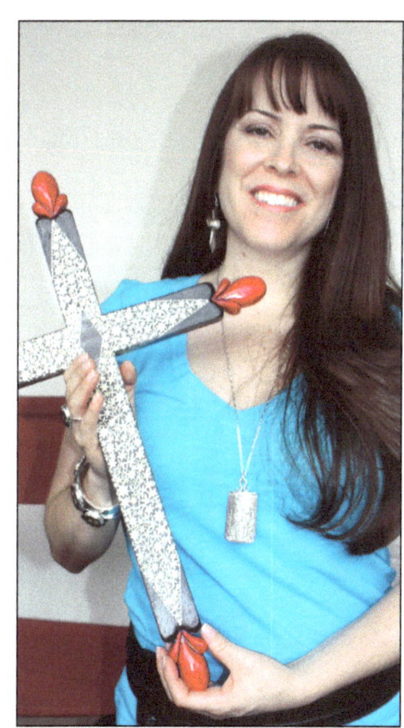

Bernadette Márquez-López
Art Form: Straw Appliqué
Contact: (505) 986-9540
Born in Española, New Mexico
Lives in Santa Fe, New Mexico
Juried into Spanish Market in 2004
Notable Awards:
Spanish Market Honorable Mention 2004,
Collaboration Award 2005 and 2009.

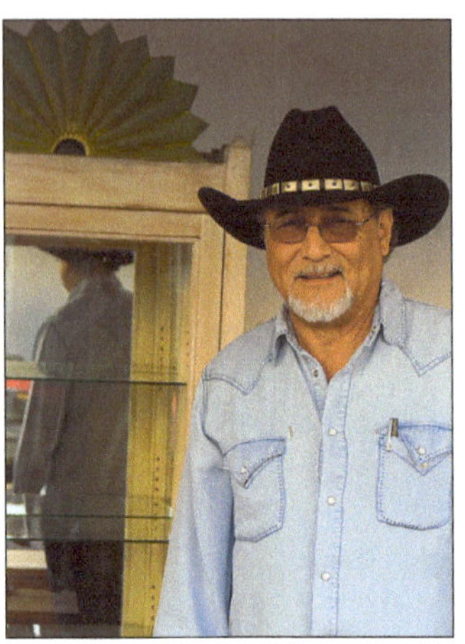

Anthony E. Mártinez

Art Form: Furniture
Contact: (505) 501-1700
Born in Santa Fe, New Mexico
Lives in Santa Fe, New Mexico
Juried into Spanish Market in 1992
Notable Awards:

Spanish Market First Place Furniture 2002/2003/2005,
Second Place Furniture 2001, Alan and Ann Vedder Award 2004,
William Field Design Award.
Española Art Festival First Place in Furniture
1992/1995/1997/2000/2001/2002.

Dominic Mártinez

Art Form: Painted *Bultos*
Contact: (505) 898-0153
Born in Española, New Mexico
Lives in Corrales, New Mexico
Juried into Spanish Market in 2005
Notable Awards:

Spanish Market Second Place Painted *Bultos* 2007,
Third Place *Bultos* en Nicho 2008.
San Felipe de Neri Santero Market Best of Show 2002.
New Mexico State Fair Honorable Mention 2001,
Third Place 2008, Third Place and
Honorable Mention 2009.

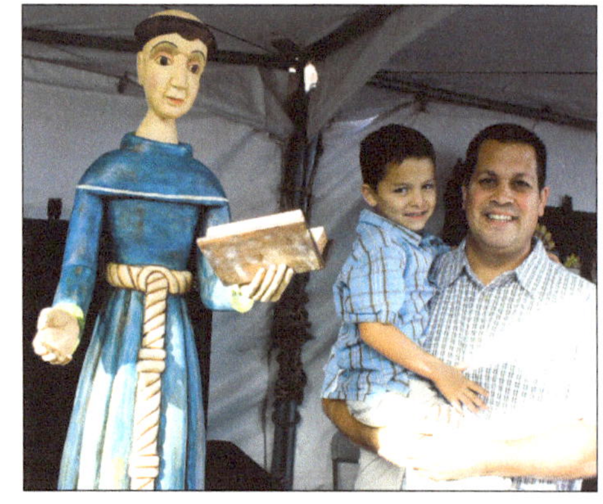

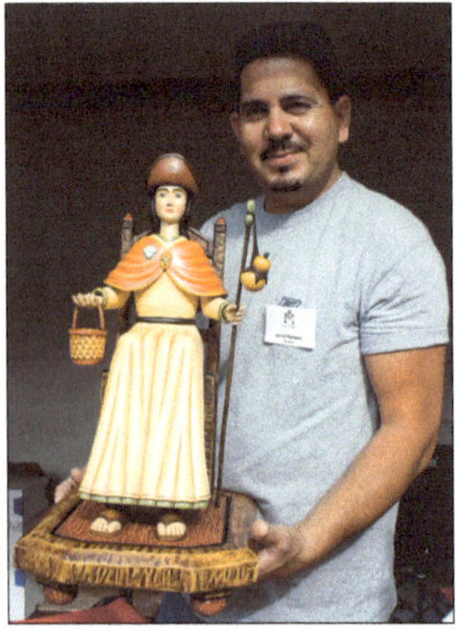

Jacob Mártinez

Art Form: Painted *Bultos*
Contact: (505) 927-8409
Born in Bernalillo, New Mexico
Lives in Dixon, New Mexico
Juried into Spanish Market in 2006
Notable Awards:

Spanish Market Second Place Painted *Bultos* 2009 and 2010.

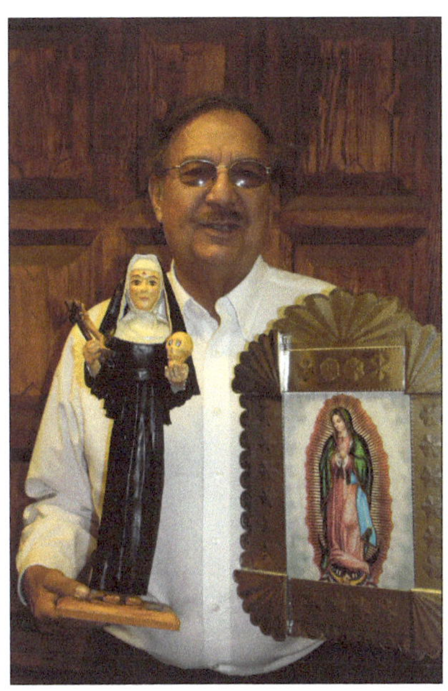

Juan D. Mártinez, Jr.
Art Form(s): Painted *Bultos*, Tinwork
Contact: (505) 929-3505
Born in San Francisco, California
Lives in Española, New Mexico
Juried into Spanish Market in 1992
Notable Awards:
Spanish Market Poster Award 2003,
Mixed Media and Tinwork Awards.

Peter L. Mártinez
Art Form: Weaving
Lives in Denver, Colorado.

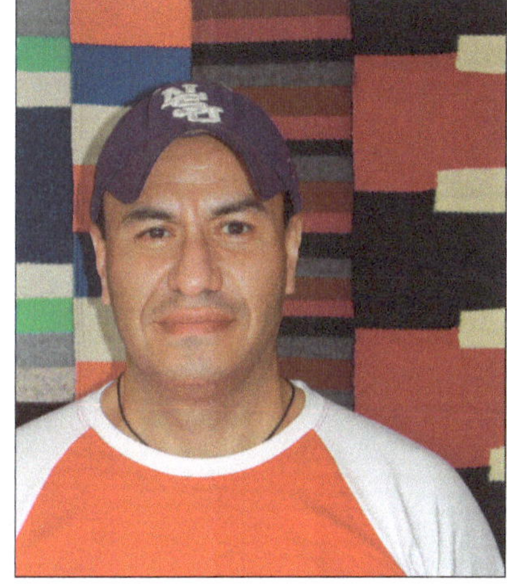

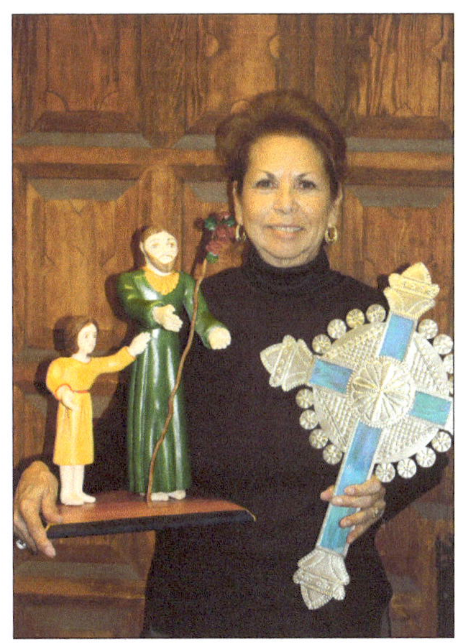

Rita Mártinez
Art Form(s): Painted *Bultos*, Tinwork
Contact: (505) 753-5166
Born in Ranchitos, New Mexico
Lives in Española, New Mexico
Juried into Spanish Market in 1992.

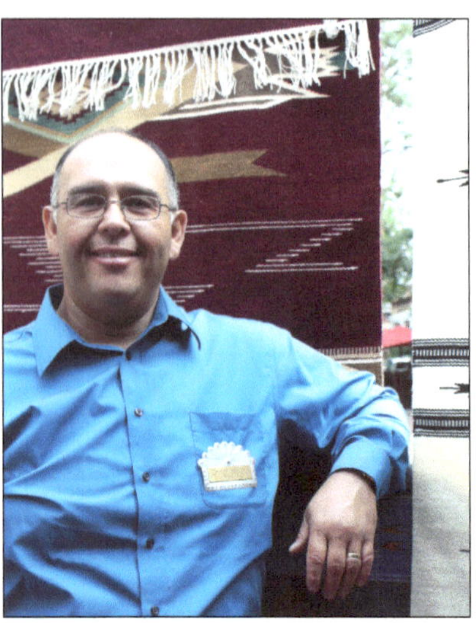

Timothy Mártinez

Art Form: Weaving
Contact: (505) 614-5897
Born in Chimayo, New Mexico
Lives in Santa Cruz, New Mexico
Juried into Spanish Market in 2002
Notable Awards:
Española Valley Art Show Best in Show 2008.

Yvonne Mártinez

Art Form: Straw Appliqué
Contact: (505) 753-3714
Born in Española, New Mexico
Lives in Corrales, New Mexico
Juried into Spanish Market in 2008
Notable Awards:
New Mexico State Fair
Honorable Mention 2009.

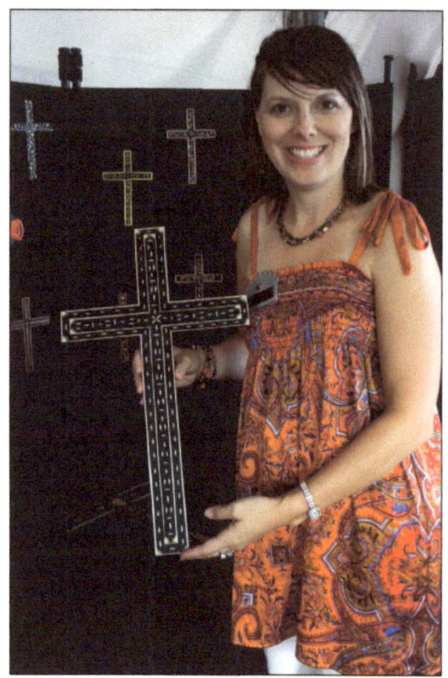

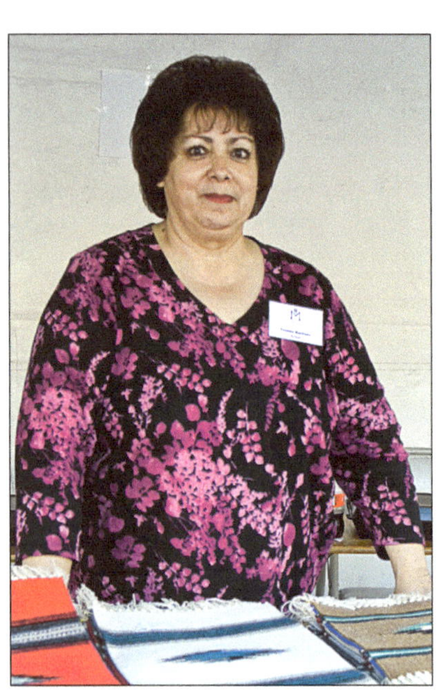

Yvonne B. Mártinez

Art Form: Weaving
Contact: (505) 753-3714
Born in Embudo, New Mexico
Lives in Española, New Mexico
Juried into Spanish Market in 1990.

Justin Gallegos Mayrant

Art Form: Tinwork
Lives in Santa Fe, New Mexico.

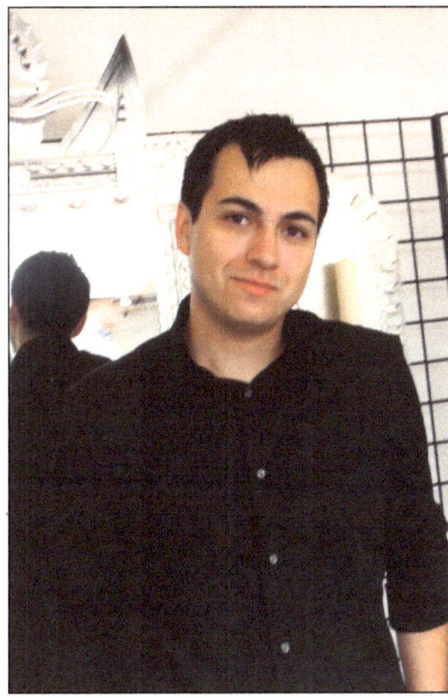

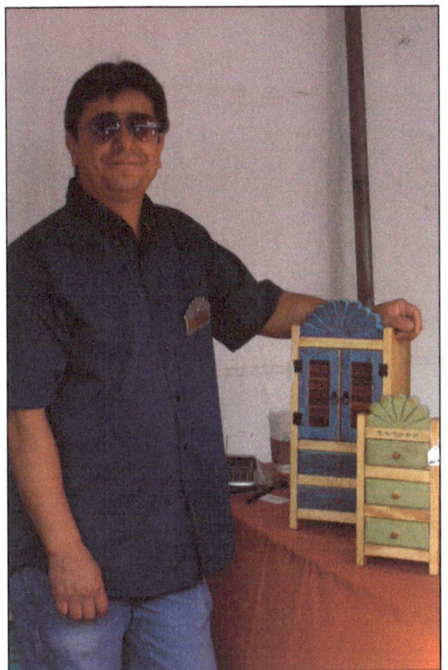

Ed Mier

Art Form: Furniture
Contact: (505) 820-1174
Born in Santa Fe, New Mexico
Lives in Santa Fe, New Mexico
Juried into Spanish Market in 1997
Notable Awards:

Spanish Market Purchase Award, Two Second Place Awards for Furniture, Lenora Curtin Paloheimo Award.

Luis Mojica

Art Form(s): Precious Metals, Pottery
Contact: (505) 254-2749
Born in Conejos County, Colorado
Lives in Albuquerque, New Mexico
Juried into Spanish Market in 1998
Notable Awards:

Spanish Market Second Place Precious Metals 1999 and 2000, Collaboration Award 2000, First Place Precious Metals 2001/2002/2005, Design Award 2010.

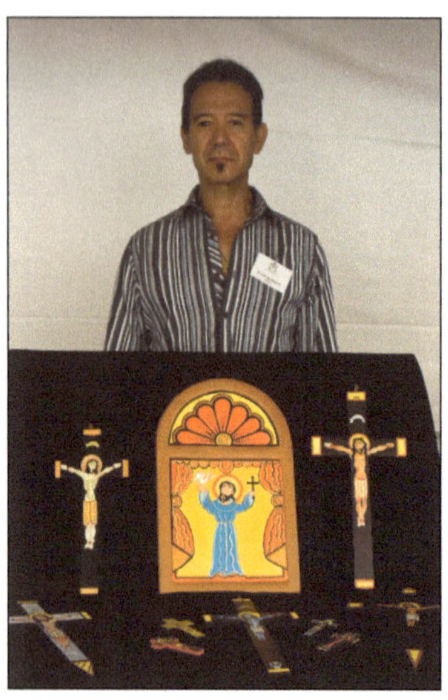

Jerry M. Mondragón

Art Form: *Retablos*
Contact: (505) 203-3755
Born in Embudo, New Mexico
Lives in Albuquerque, New Mexico
Juried into Spanish Market in 1990
Notable Awards:

Spanish Market First Place *Retablos* 1996, Purchase Award 1997.
New Mexico State Fair Third Place 1999, Second Place 2004.

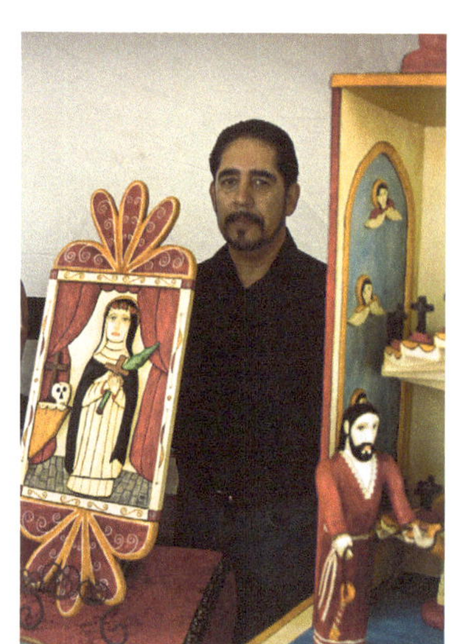

Margarito R. Mondragón

Art Form(s): *Retablos*, Relief Carving, *Bultos*
Contact: (505) 690-1916
Born in Ocate, New Mexico
Lives in Las Vegas, New Mexico
Juried into Spanish Market in 1996
Notable Awards:
Spanish Market Design Award 2001, Second Place Altar Screens 2002, Director's Choice Award and Mixed Media Award 2003, Poster Award 2006, Second Place *Bultos* en Nicho 2009, People's Choice Award 2010.

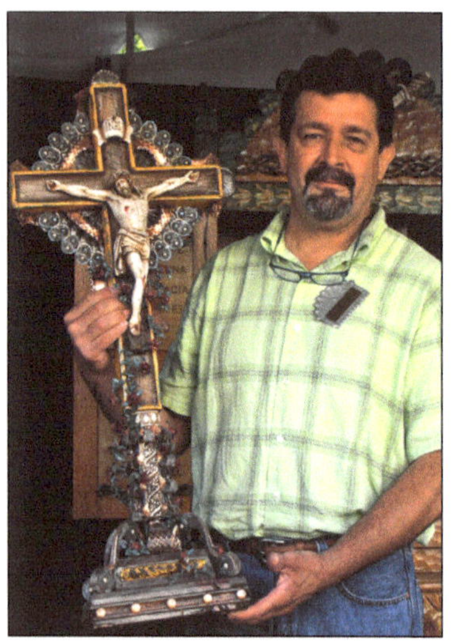

Arturo Montaño

Art Form: Bone Carving
Contact: (505) 685-4618
Born in Santa Fe, New Mexico
Lives in Abiquiu, New Mexico
Juried into Spanish Market in 2002
Notable Awards:

Spanish Market First Place Tinwork in 2003 and 2007, People's Choice Award 2004, Second Place *Bultos* en Nicho 2007, Second Place Painted *Bultos* 2008.
Festival of the Masters, Orlando FL, Second Place Sculpture 2002.
New Mexico State Fair Best of Show 2004.
Fiesta de Colores Best of Show 2001 and 2006.

Barbara A. Montaño
Art Form: Tinwork
Contact: (505) 901-1800
Born in Hernandez, New Mexico
Lives in Española, New Mexico
Juried into Spanish Market in 1998
Notable Awards:
Spanish Market Second Place 2005.
New Mexico State Fair Second Place 2006.
El Rancho de las Golondrinas Award for Excellence in Traditional Tinwork 2005.

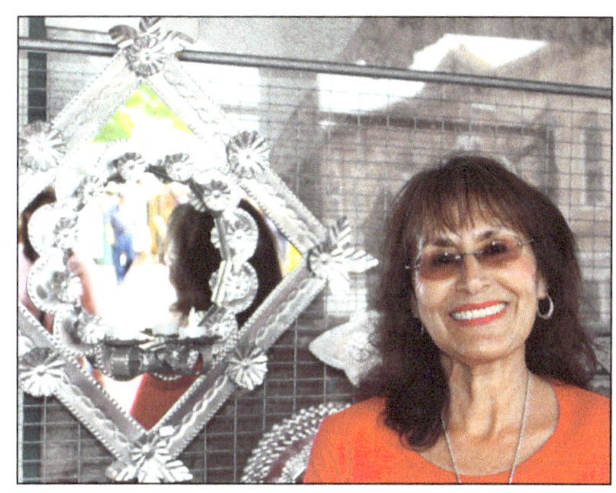

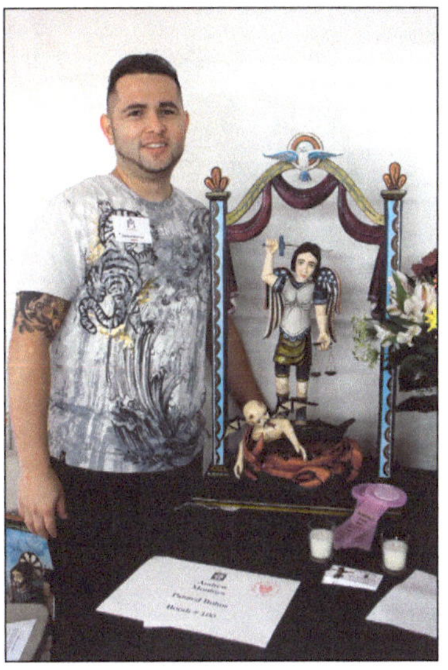

Andrew Montoya
Art Form: Painted *Bultos*, *Retablos*
Contact: (505) 470-6202
Born in Santa Fe, New Mexico
Lives in Santa Fe, New Mexico
Juried into Spanish Market in 2005
Notable Awards:
Spanish Market Third Place Painted *Bultos* 2006 and 2008, Collaboration Award and Second Place *Bultos* 2007, First Place Painted *Bultos* 2009, Archbishop's Award 2010.

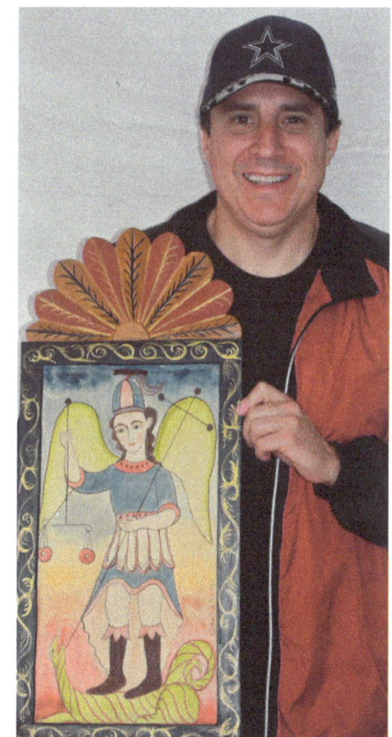

Gilbert Montoya
Art Form(s): Painted *Bultos*, *Retablos*
Lives in Santa Fe, New Mexico.

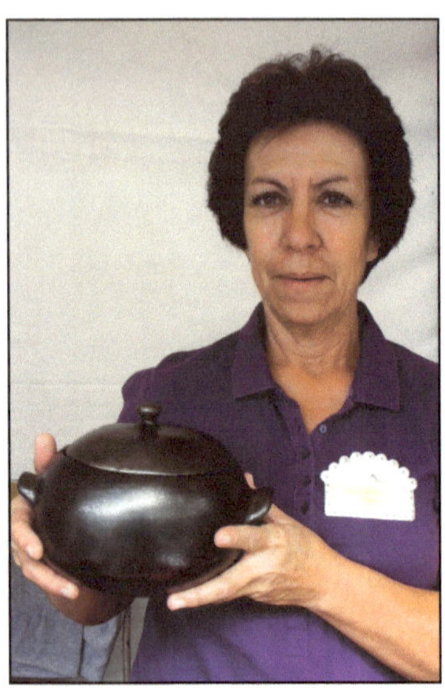

Annette Morfín
Art Form: Pottery
Lives in Youngsville, New Mexico.

Jason R. Mossman
Art Form: Furniture
Lives in Santa Fe, New Mexico.

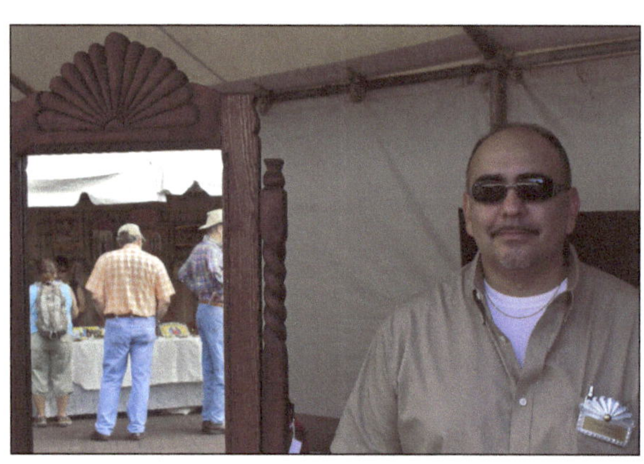

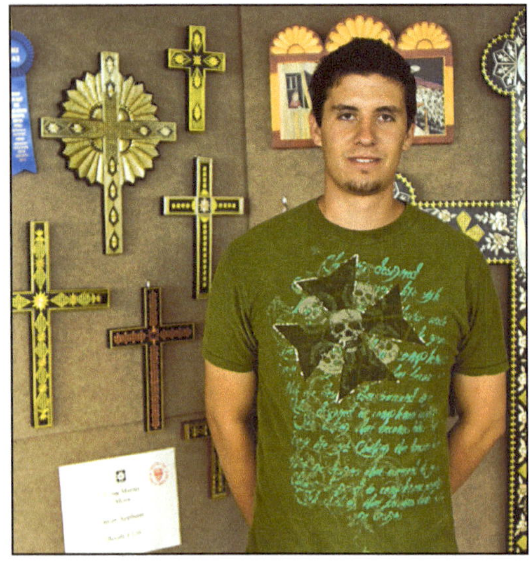

Craig Moya
Art Form: Straw Appliqué
Contact: (505) 466-1544
Born in Santa Fe, New Mexico
Lives in Galisteo, New Mexico
Juried into Spanish Market in 2006
Notable Awards:
- Spanish Market Bienvenidos Award 2006,
- First Place Straw Appliqué 2010.
- New Mexico State Fair First Place 2008/2009/2010.

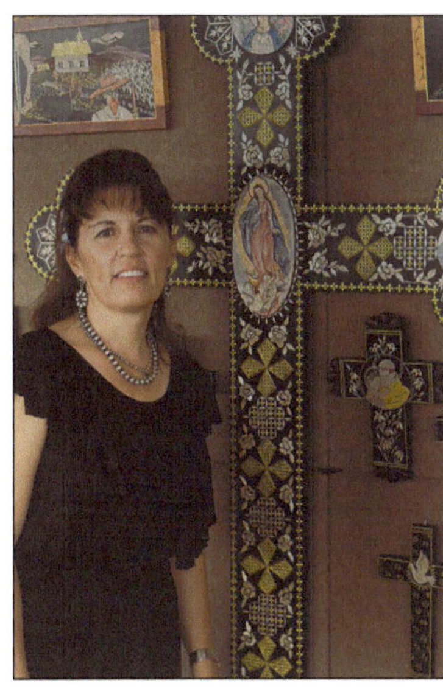

Jean Anaya Moya

Art Form(s): *Retablos*, Hide Painting, Straw Appliqué
Contact: (505) 466-1544
Born in Santa Fe, New Mexico
Lives in Galisteo, New Mexico
Juried into Spanish Market in 1998
Notable Awards:
Spanish Market Boeckman Award, Judges Choice Award 1999,
Second Place Altar Screens 2003,
Honorable Mention Straw Appliqué 2006,
E Boyd Award and First Place Mixed Media 2001/2004/2007,
Alan and Ann Vedder Award and Best of Show Award 2005,
E Boyd Award 2008.
New Mexico State Fair De Colores Award 2000,
Best of Show Award 2005, Second Place Traditional Folk Art 2006,
First Place *Bultos* and Third Place Traditional Folk Art 2008,
First Place Straw Appliqué 2010.

Adán Eduardo Ortega

Art Form: Pottery
Contact: (505) 747-1548
Born in Hernandez, New Mexico
Lives in Española, New Mexico
Juried into Spanish Market in 1995
Notable Awards:
Spanish Market Utilitarian Award 1995,
Honorable Mention Award 2006.
New Mexico State Fair First Place Awards
1996/2000/2006/2007, Third Place Award 2005,
Honorable Mention 2006.
Santa Fe 400 Years Anniversary
"Legacy and Legend Award" 1610–2010.

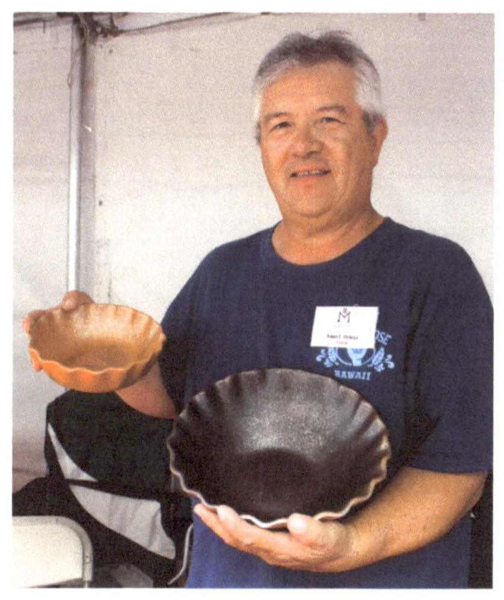

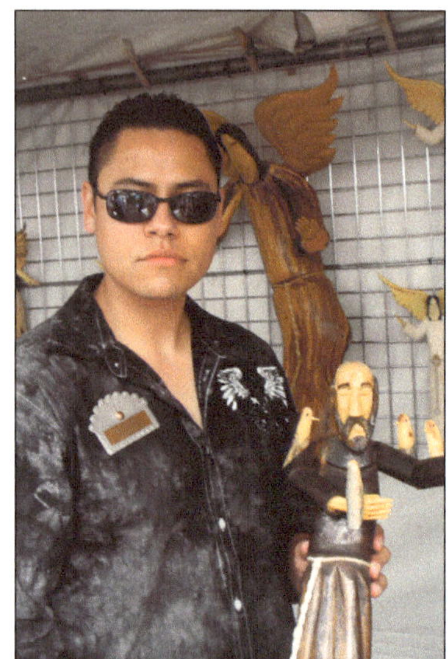

Antonio P. Ortega

Art Form: Woodcarving
Contact: (505) 231-1714
Born in Santa Fe, New Mexico
Lives in Santa Fe, New Mexico
Juried into Spanish Market in 2007
Notable Awards:
Spanish Market José Dolores López Award,
Second Place Award 2007 and 2008.

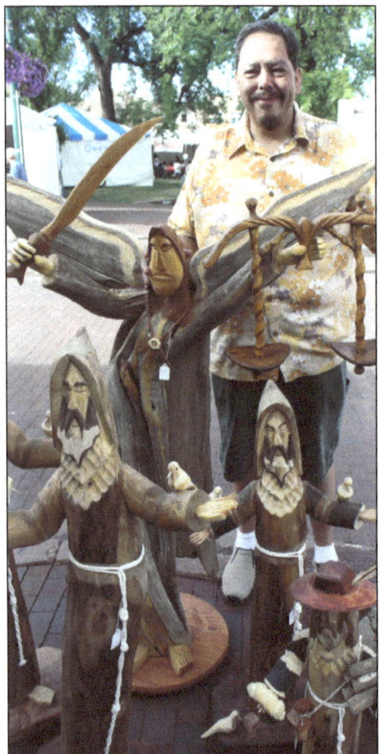

Peter Ortega

Art Form: Woodcarving
Contact: (505) 920-6983
Born in Tesuque, New Mexico
Lives in Santa Fe, New Mexico
Juried into Spanish Market in 1998
Notable Awards:
Spanish Market Second Place Unpainted *Bultos*, 2001, Third Place Unpainted *Bultos* 2009, Woodcarving Award 2010.

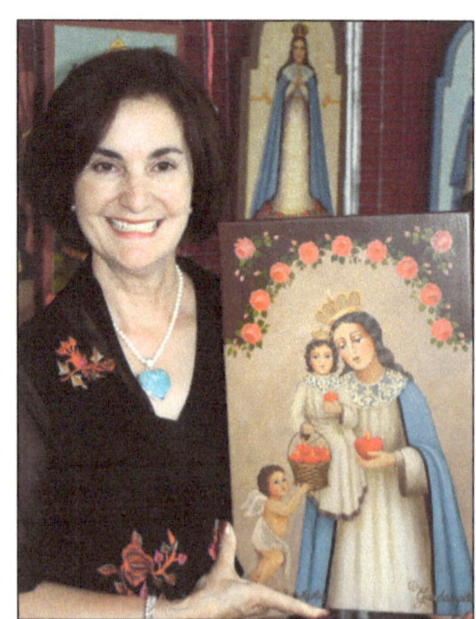

Guadalupita Ortiz

Art Form: *Retablos*
Contact: (505) 275-3552
Born in Santa Fe, New Mexico
Lives in Albuquerque, New Mexico
Juried into Spanish Market in 1979
Notable Awards:
Spanish Market Florence Dibell Bartlett Award 1989 and 1991,
First Place Mixed Media 1994.
New Mexico State Fair First Place Ribbon 1995/1997/2002,
Second Place Ribbon 1995/1996/1997/2007,
Woman's Award of Excellence by De Colores 2002,
Laureate of the Mother Teresa Award 2005.
Feria Artistica First Place Award 2000, Second Place Award 2001.

Sabinita López Ortiz

Art Form: Woodcarving
Contact: (505) 351-4572
Born in Córdova, New Mexico
Lives in Córdova, New Mexico
Juried into Spanish Market in 1984
Notable Awards:
Spanish Market William Field Design Award,
Master's Award for Lifetime Achievement 2000.
Smithsonian Heritage Award.
Colorado Spring Museum Award Best *Bultos*.
Fort Mason Museum Best Design Award.

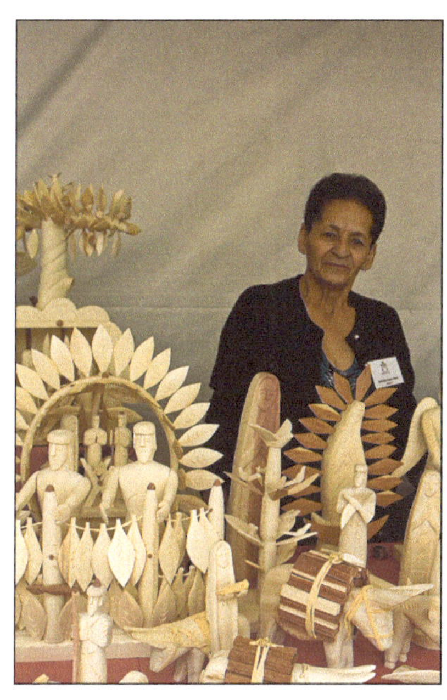

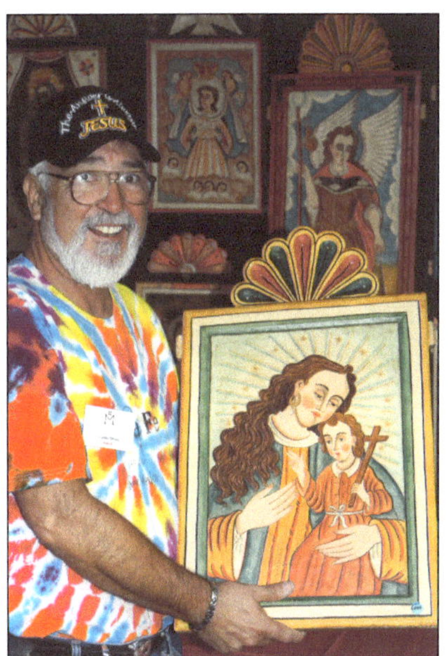

Alcario Otero

Art Form(s): Painted *Bultos*, *Retablos*, Relief Carving
Contact: (505) 866-5948
Born in Silver City, New Mexico
Lives in Los Lentes, New Mexico
Juried into Spanish Market in 1999
Notable Awards:

Spanish Market Second Place Altar Screens 2001 and 2009,
First Place Small *Retablos* 2002 and 2010,
Our Lady of Guadalupe Award 2003/2004/2010,
Honorable Mention Large *Retablos* 2006,
First Place Small *Retablos* 2007/2009/2010,
Hispanic Heritage Award, Archbishop's Award and Purchase Award 2007, Second Place Small *Retablos* 2008 and 2010,
First Place Large *Retablos* 2008.

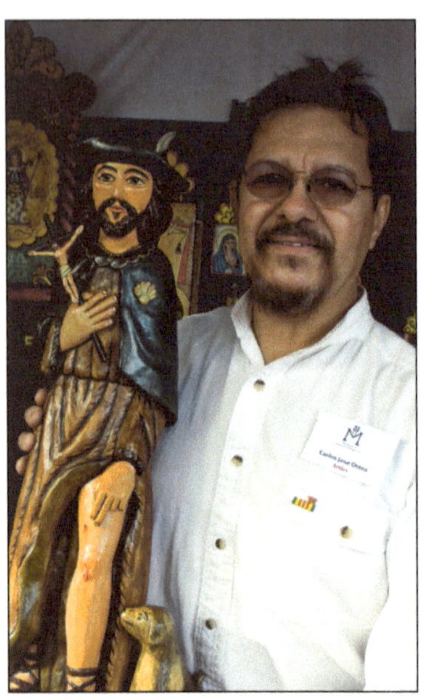

Carlos José Otero

Art Form(s): Painted *Bultos*, *Retablos*, Relief Carving
Contact: (505) 792-0393
Born in El Cerro, New Mexico
Lives in Albuquerque, New Mexico
Juried into Spanish Market in 1997
Notable Awards:

Spanish Market Second Place twice, Design Award.
New Mexico State Fair Best of Show twice.
Grants New Mexico Art Show Best of Show.
Nuestra Senora de Loreto Judges Choice Award.

Nicolas R. Otero

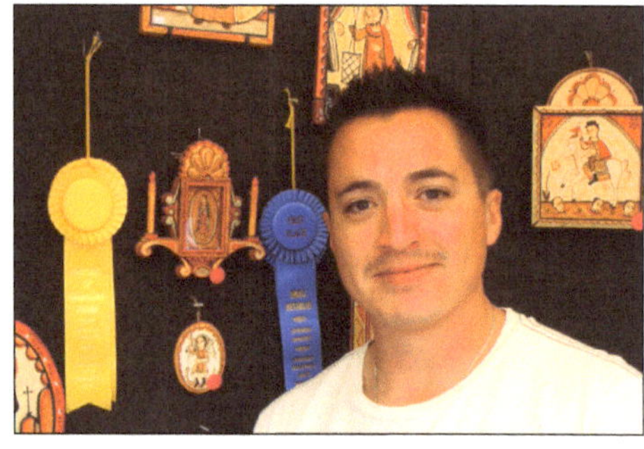

Art Form: *Retablos*
Contact: (505) 866-5948
Born in Silver City, New Mexico
Lives in Los Lentes, New Mexico
Juried into Spanish Market in 1998
Notable Awards:
Spanish Market Purchase Award 1998, First Place Small *Retablos* 2002/2007/2009/2010, First Place Large *Retablos* 2005, First Place Altar Screen 2007, Archbishop's Award and Purchase Award 2007, Our Lady of Guadalupe Award 2003/2004/2010.

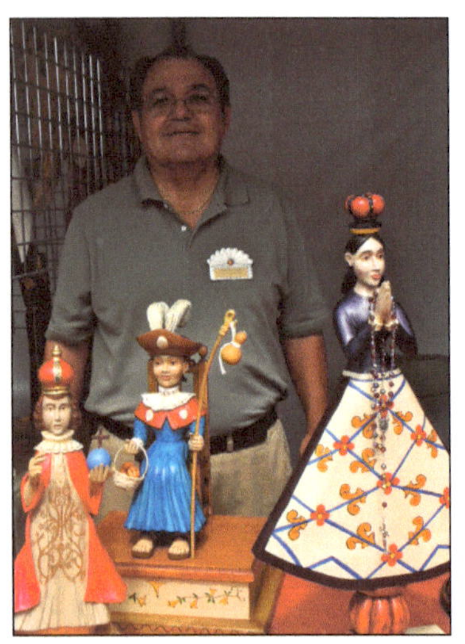

Rodolfo Parga

Art Form: Painted *Bultos*
Contact: (505) 899-1486
Born in El Paso, Texas
Lives in Albuquerque, New Mexico
Juried into Spanish Market in 2008
Notable Awards:

Spanish Market Bienvenidos Award.
New Mexico State Fair First Place Painted *Bultos* 2007,
Honorable Mention Painted *Bultos* 2006.

Federico Prudencio

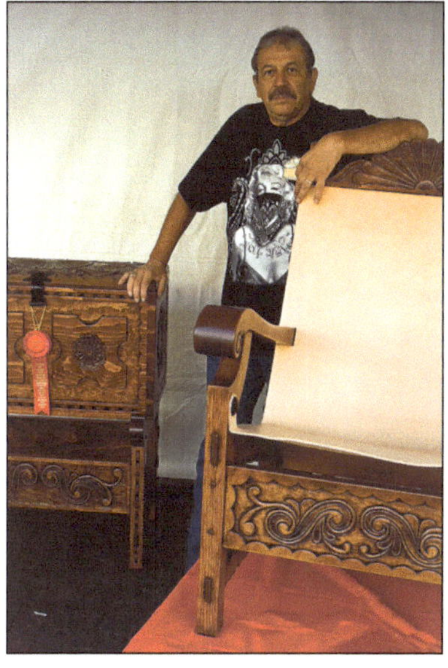

Art Form: Furniture
Contact: (505) 710-8593
Born in Albuquerque, New Mexico
Lives in Albuquerque, New Mexico
Juried into Spanish Market in 1991
Notable Awards:
Spanish Market Best of Show Award 2002, Leonora Curtin Paloheimo Award for Excellence, First Place 2001 and 2008, Second Place 2004//2006/2009/2010, Utilitarian Award 2003, Our Lady of Guadalupe Award 2008, Collections Committee Award 2009.

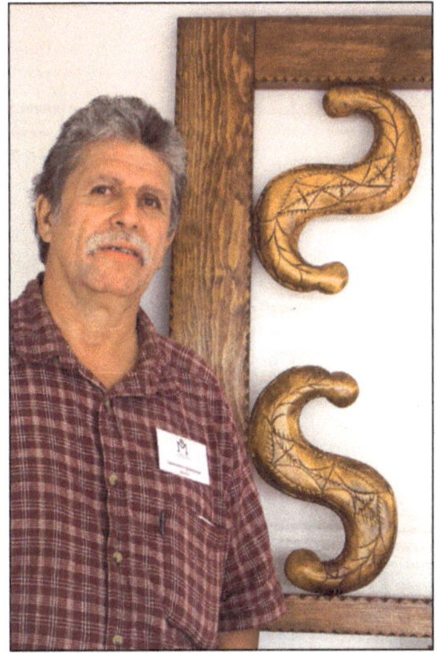

Lawrence Quintana

Art Form: Furniture
Contact: (505) 795-6756
Born in Santa Fe, New Mexico
Lives in Santa Fe, New Mexico
Juried into Spanish Market in 1989
Notable Awards:

Spanish Market Bienvenidos and Purchase Award 1989,
José Delores López Award.
New Mexico State Fair Honorable Mention 1998.
Gene Autry Museum Purchase Award 1990 and 1991.

Carlos A. Rael

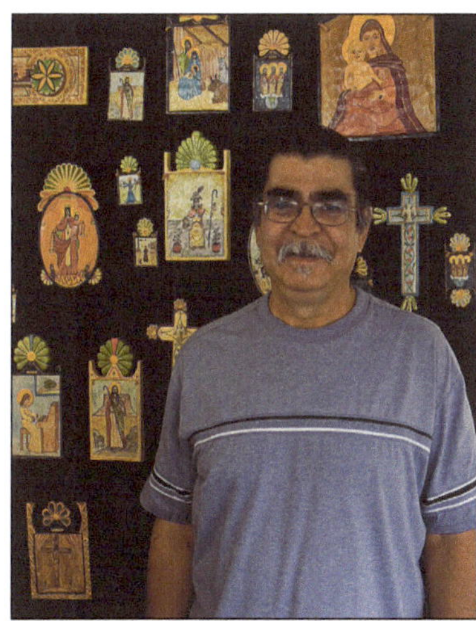

Art Form(s): *Retablos*, Painted *Bultos*
Contact: (575) 758-7503
Born in Santa Fe, New Mexico
Lives in Ranchos de Taos, New Mexico
Juried into Spanish Market in 1999
Notable Awards:
Spanish Market Poster Award 1999, Honorable Mention *Bultos* 2003. Taos Invites Taos Best of Show Award and Best of Santos Award 2002, Living Master Award 2008.

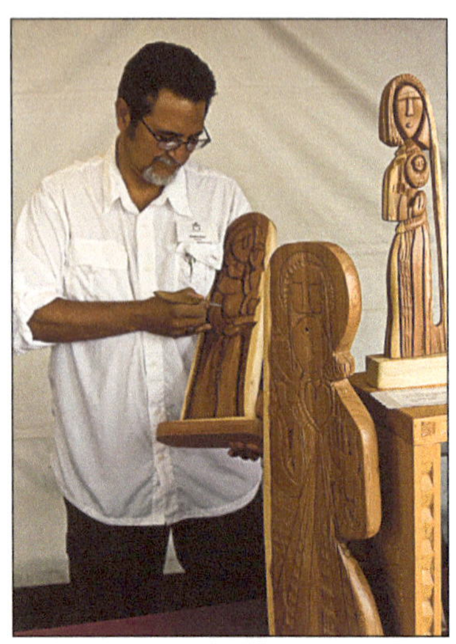

Daniel L. Rael

Art Form(s): Relief Carving, Woodcarving
Contact: (575) 751-0547
Born in Embudo, New Mexico
Lives in Taos, New Mexico
Juried into Spanish Market in 1998
Notable Awards:

Spanish Market Second Place Unpainted *Bultos* 2006.
Taylor Museum Purchase Award 2000.

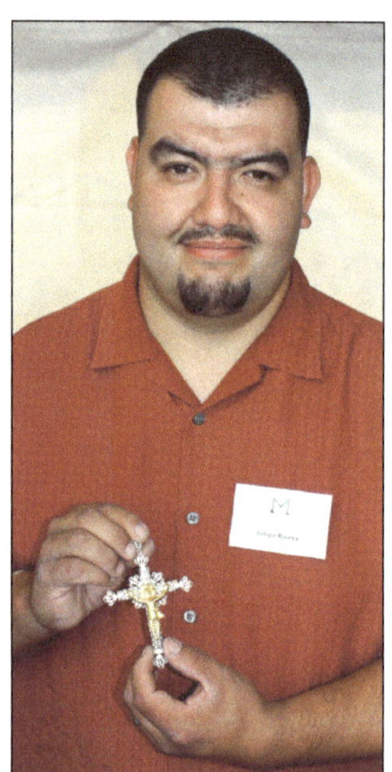

Felipe Rivera

Art Form: Precious Metals
Contact: (505) 249-8226
Born in Albuquerque, New Mexico
Lives in Albuquerque, New Mexico
Juried into Spanish Market in 2010
Notable Awards:
New Mexico State Fair First Place Precious Metals 2010, Third Place *Bultos* 2010.

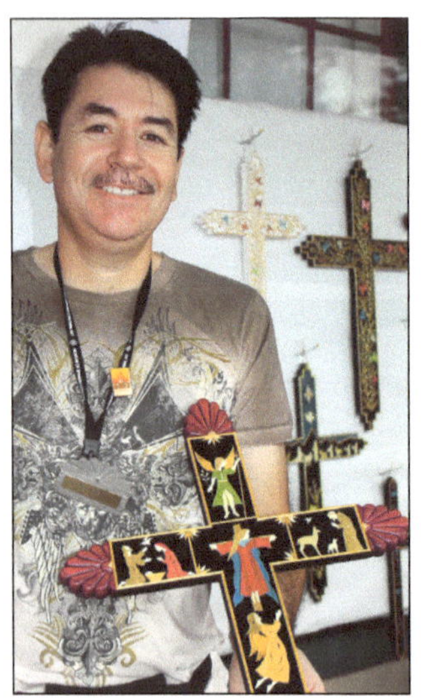

Mel Rivera

Art Form: Straw Appliqué
Contact: (505) 455-7943
Born in Santa Fe, New Mexico
Lives in Nambe, New Mexico
Juried into Spanish Market in 1988
Notable Awards:

Spanish Market Purchase Award, Collaboration Award, First Place, Second Place, E Boyd Award, Alan and Ann Vedder Award.
US West New Directions Award.
New Mexico State Fair First/Second/Third/Honorable Mention Awards, De Colores Purchase Award.
Denver Spanish Market First Place Award.
Taylor Museum Purchase Award;
Heard Museum Spanish Market People's Choice Award.

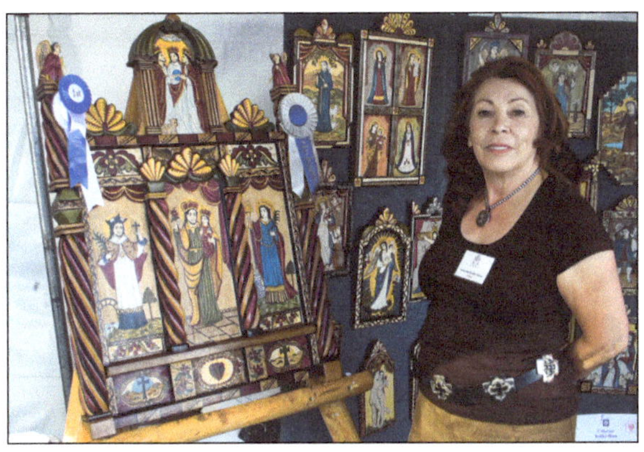

Catherine Robles-Shaw

Art Form(s): *Retablos*, *Bultos*
Contact: 303-258-0544
Born in Denver, CO
Lives in Nederland, CO
Juried into Spanish Market in 1995
Notable Awards:

Spanish Market Distinguished Artist Award 2000, First Place Altar Screens 2001/2002/2003/2004/2005 /2006/2009, First Place Large *Retablos* 2003, Purchase Award 2003 and 2004, Our Lady of Guadalupe Award 2005, Boeckman Award 2009. New Mexico Secretary of State Dedication and Service Award 2000. Boulder County CO Multi-Cultural Award Artist of the Year 2007.

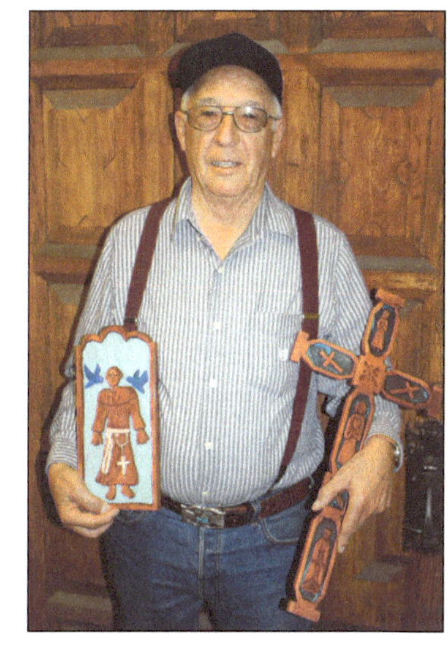

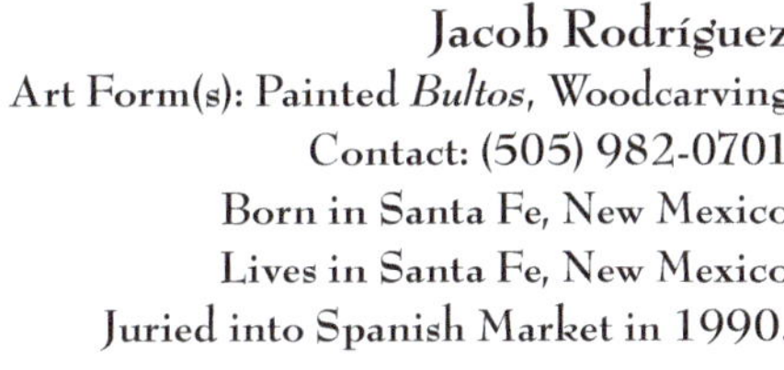

Jacob Rodríguez

Art Form(s): Painted *Bultos*, Woodcarving
Contact: (505) 982-0701
Born in Santa Fe, New Mexico
Lives in Santa Fe, New Mexico
Juried into Spanish Market in 1990.

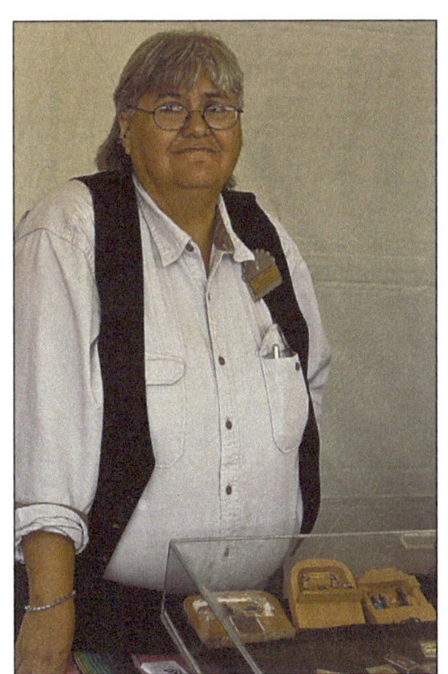

Tomasita Rodríguez

Art Form(s): Woodcarving, Inlaid Crosses, Nichos, Painted *Bultos*
Contact: (505) 795-1647
Born in Santa Fe, New Mexico
Lives in Santa Fe, New Mexico
Juried into Spanish Market in 1983
Notable Awards:

Spanish Market Second Place Mixed Media 2007.

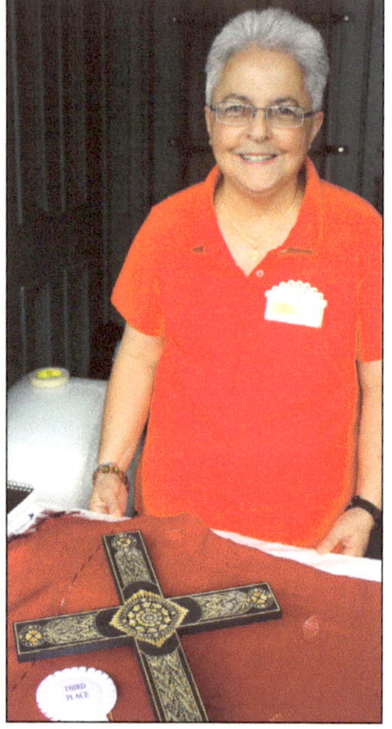

Vicki Rodríguez

Art Form: Straw Appliqué
Contact: (505) 989-7493
Born in Santa Fe, New Mexico
Lives in Santa Fe, New Mexico
Juried into Spanish Market in 1980
Notable Awards:
Spanish Market First Place 1984/1999/2002/2006, Purchase Award 1997, Honorable Mention 1998, Second Place 2003 and 2010, Design Award 2007, Third Place 2010.

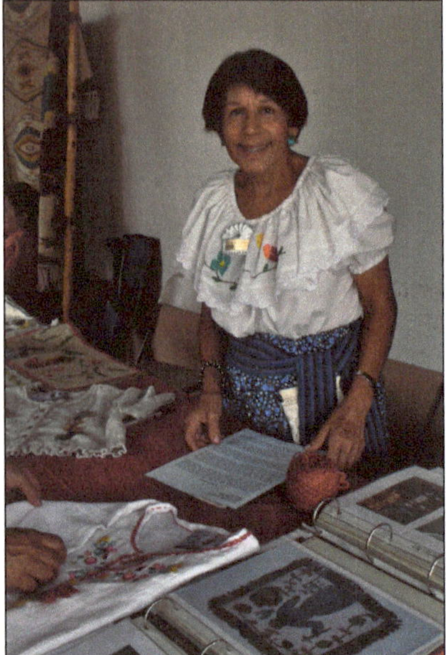

Victoria Lucero Rodríguez

Art Form: Colcha Embroidery
Contact: (505) 986-1267
Born in Puerto de Luna of Santa Rosa, New Mexico
Lives in Santa Fe, New Mexico
Juried into Spanish Market in 1998
Notable Awards:

- Spanish Market Collaboration Award 2000.
- New Mexico State Fair two awards.

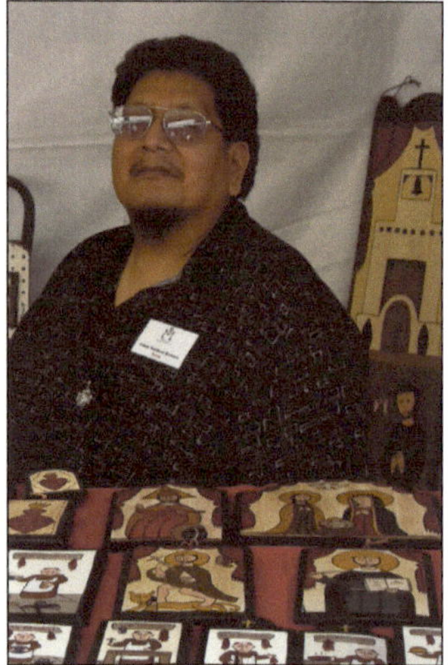

Adam Matthew Romero

Art Form: *Retablos*
Contact: (505) 753-6610
Born in Santa Fe, New Mexico
Lives in Española, New Mexico
Juried into Spanish Market in 1990.

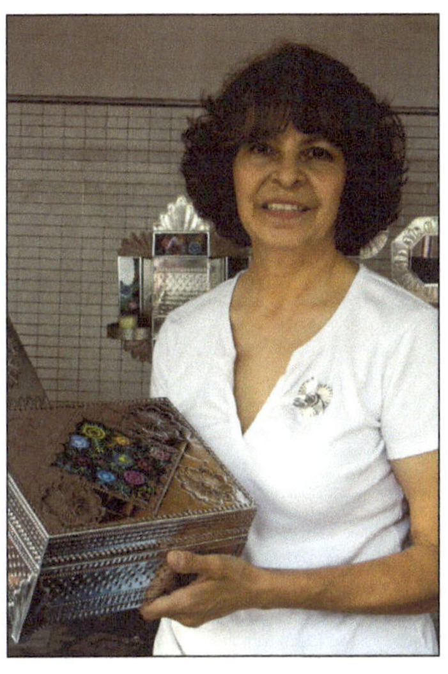

Cleo Romero

Art Form: Tinwork
Contact: (505) 753-2143
Born in Santa Fe, New Mexico
Lives in Nambe, New Mexico
Juried into Spanish Market in 2006
Notable Awards:
Spanish Market First Place 2006/2008/2009,
Honorable Mention 2007,
First and Second Place and Purchase Award 2008.
New Mexico State Fair Best of Show 2006, Third Place 2008.

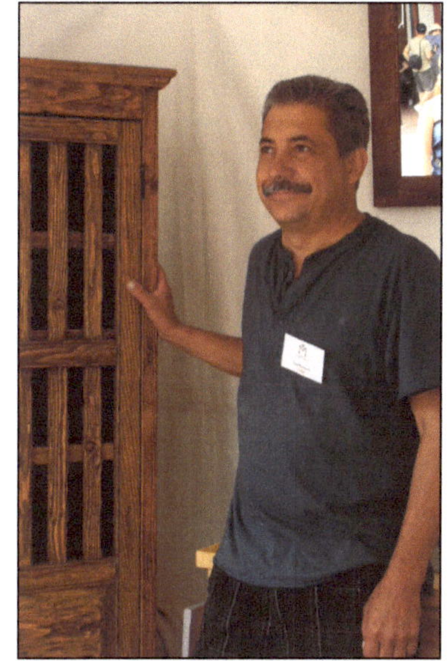

Fred Romero

Art Form: Furniture
Contact: (505) 753-6270
Born in Española, New Mexico
Lives in Santa Cruz, New Mexico
Juried into Spanish Market in 1989
Notable Awards:
Spanish Market Second Place 1999, First Place 2000.
Española Tri-Cultural Arts Best of Category 1986, Best of Show 1987.
New Mexico State Fair First Place 1991.
New Mexico Woodworker's Exhibition First Place 1996.
Santa Fe Design Week First and Third Place 2003.
Style New Mexico Best of Show 2002.

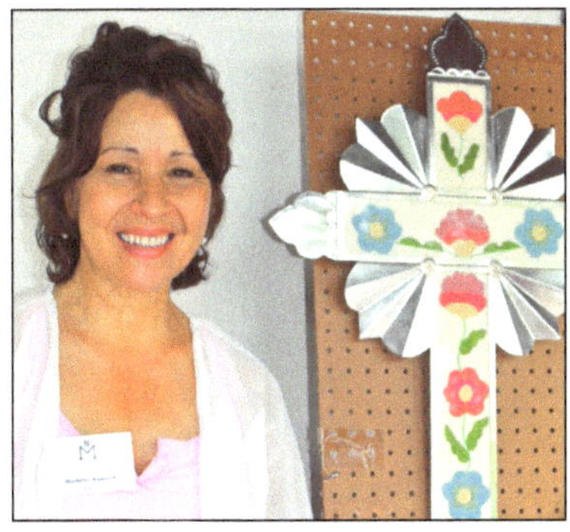

Michelle Romero

Art Form: Tinwork
Contact: (505) 982-4676
Born in Santa Fe, New Mexico
Lives in Santa Fe, New Mexico
Juried into Spanish Market in 2010.

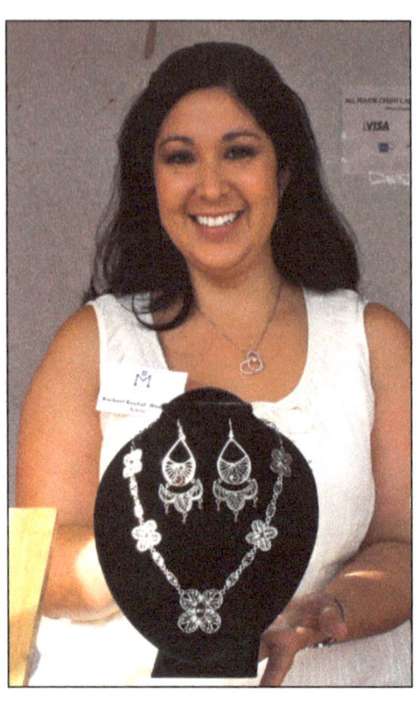

Rachel Roybal-Montoya

Art Form: Precious Metals
Contact: (505) 570-6555
Born in Pojoaque, New Mexico
Lives in Arroyo Seco, New Mexico
Juried into Spanish Market in 2010.

Cleo Salazar

Art Form: Weaving
Contact: (575) 638-5543
Born in Coyote, New Mexico
Lives in Coyote, New Mexico
Juried into Spanish Market in 1980.

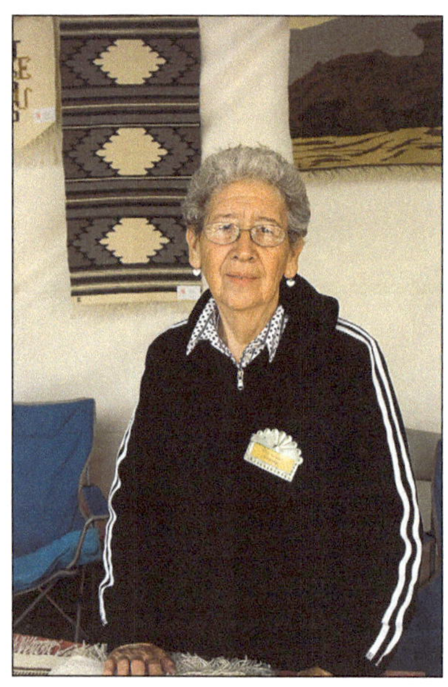

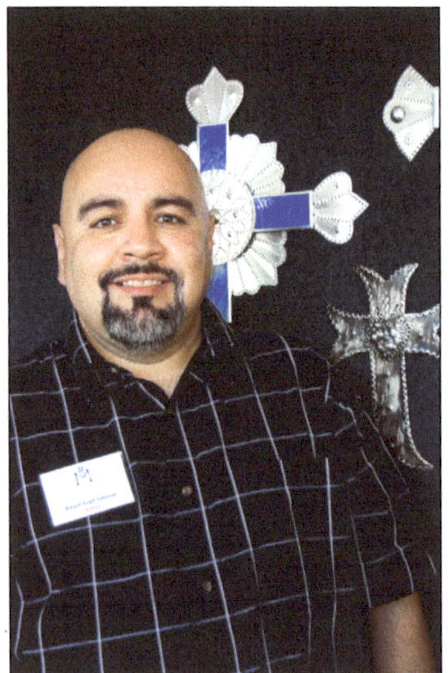

David Vigil Salazar

Art Form: Tinwork
Contact: (505) 753-4894
Born in Fairview, New Mexico
Lives in Santa Cruz, New Mexico
Juried into Spanish Market in 1999
Notable Awards:

Spanish Market Second Place 2000 and 2001, Alan and Ann Vedder Award Collaboration 2002, Honorable Mention 2004.
Española Valley Arts Festival Second Place 1999/2000/2001, First Place 2002 and 2003, Best of Show Collaboration 2001, First Place Collaboration 2004.
Española Valley Arts Festival Second Place Poster Collaboration 2003.
New Mexico State Fair First and Second Place 2002.
Tesoro Foundation Spanish Market First Place 2005, First Place Collaboration 2006.

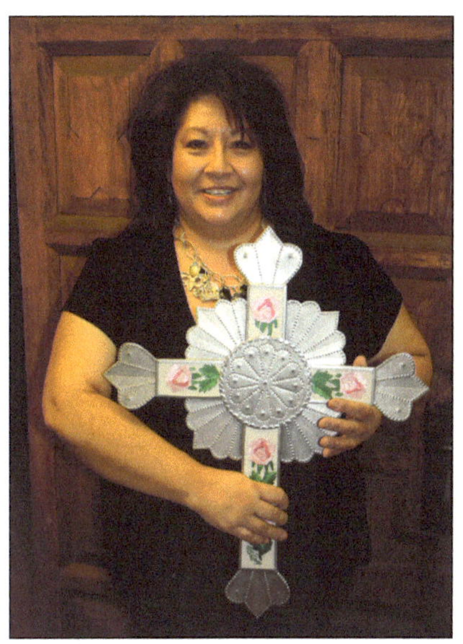

Gina Vigil Salazar

Art Form: Cocha Embroidery
Contact: (505) 753-4894
Born in Denver, Colorado
Lives in Santa Cruz, New Mexico
Juried into Spanish Market in 2002
Notable Awards:

Spanish Market Alan and Ann Vedder Award Collaboration 2002.
Española Valley Arts Festival Second Place Fiber Arts 1999,
First Place Fiber Arts 2000 and 2001, Third Place Fiber Arts 2002,
Second Place Poster Collaboration Award 2003.
New Mexico State Fair Second Place and Honorable Mention 2002.
Tesoro Foundation Spanish Market Second Place Colcha 2005,
First Place Collaboration 2006.

Jacob Salazar

Art Form: Woodcarving
Lives in Albuquerque, New Mexico.

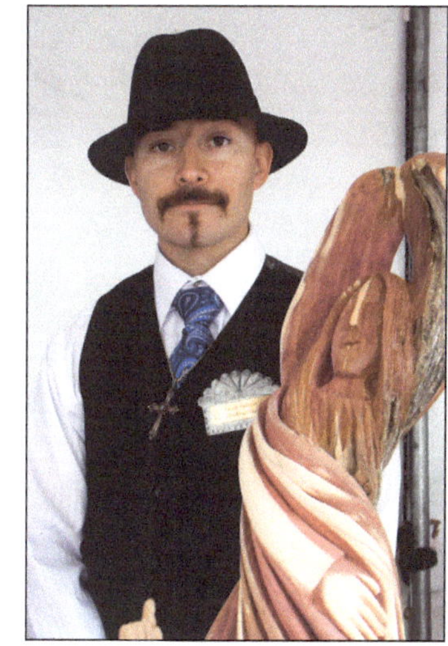

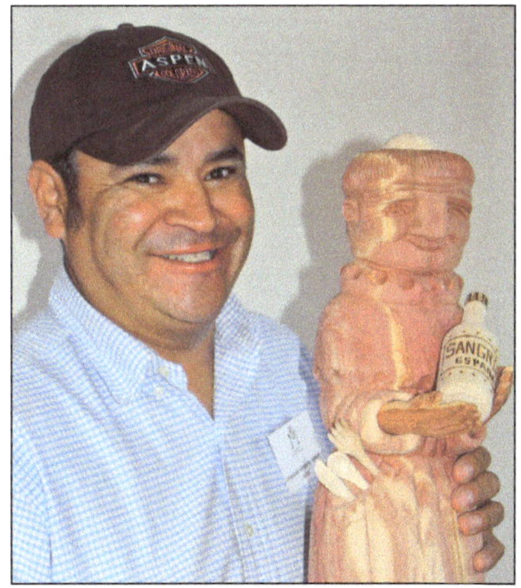

Leonardo Gregorio Salazar

Art Form: Woodcarving
Contact: (505) 550-7387
Born in Taos, New Mexico
Lives in Taos, New Mexico
Juried into Spanish Market in 1972
Notable Awards:

Spanish Market Leo G. Salazar Memorial Award.
Taos Invites Taos Best of Show 2000.

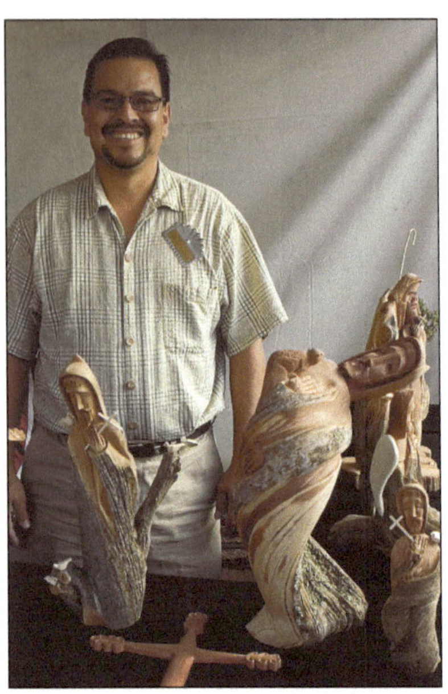

Ricardo P. Salazar

Art Form: Woodcarving
Contact: (575) 741-1963
Born in Taos, New Mexico
Lives in El Prado, New Mexico
Juried into Spanish Market in 1990
Notable Awards:

Spanish Market First Place Unpainted *Bultos* 1998, Honorable Mention Unpainted *Bultos* 1999 and 2000, Purchase Award 2000.
Fiesta de Colores Best of Show 1998.

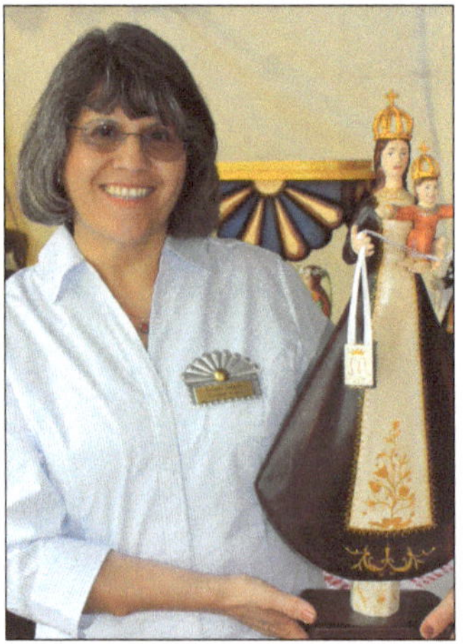

Rosalie Salazar

Art Form: Painted *Bultos*
Lives in Española, New Mexico.

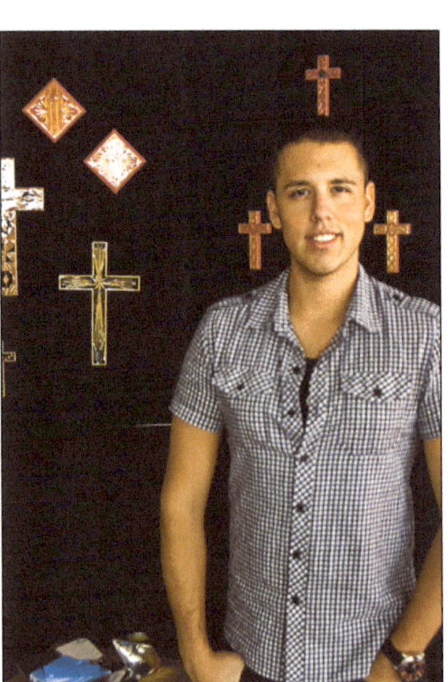

Tomás Salazar y Weiler

Art Form: Straw Appliqué
Contact: (505) 288-0016
Born in Santa Fe, New Mexico
Lives in Corrales, New Mexico
Juried into Spanish Market in 2007
Notable Awards:

Spanish Market Bienvenidos Award and Collaboration Award 2007.

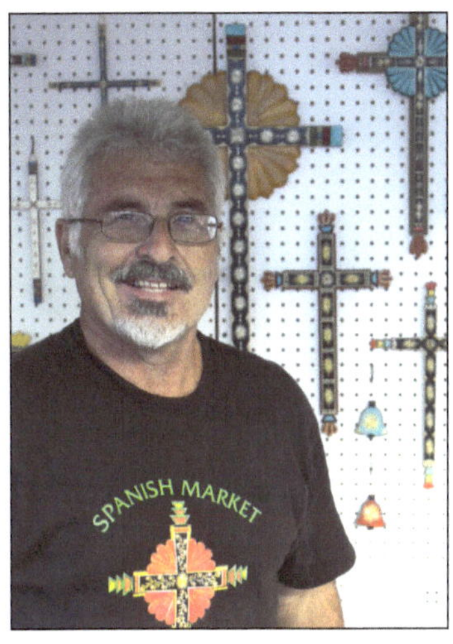

Charlie Sánchez, Jr.

Art Form: Straw Appliqué
Contact: (505) 865-5409
Born in Albuquerque, New Mexico
Lives in Tome, New Mexico
Juried into Spanish Market in 1993
Notable Awards:

Spanish Market Bienvenidos Award 1993, Archbishop's Award, Purchase Award two times, First Place Mixed Media three times, Florence Dibell Bartlett Award.
New Mexico State Fair First Place.
New Mexico National Poster Award.

Vanessa M. Sánchez

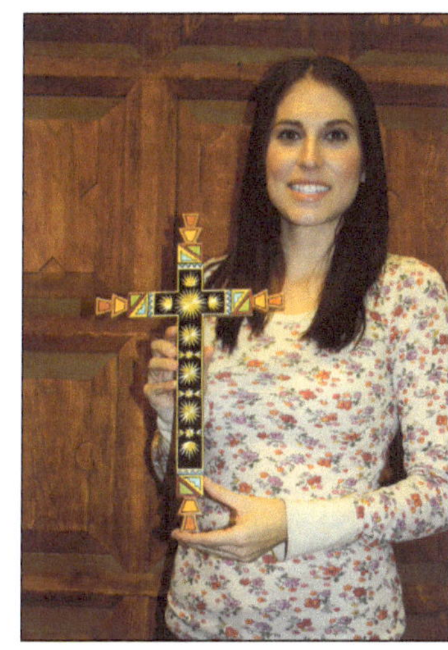

Art Form: Straw Appliqué
Contact: (505) 865-5409
Born in Tome, New Mexico
Lives in Tome, New Mexico
Juried into Spanish Market in 2001
Notable Awards:

Spanish Market Honorable Mention Mixed Media 2001, Second Place Mixed Media 2002.
San Felipe de Neri Market Best of Show Grand Prize 2002.
New Mexico State Fair Third Place 2005 and 2006, Honorable Mention 2007.

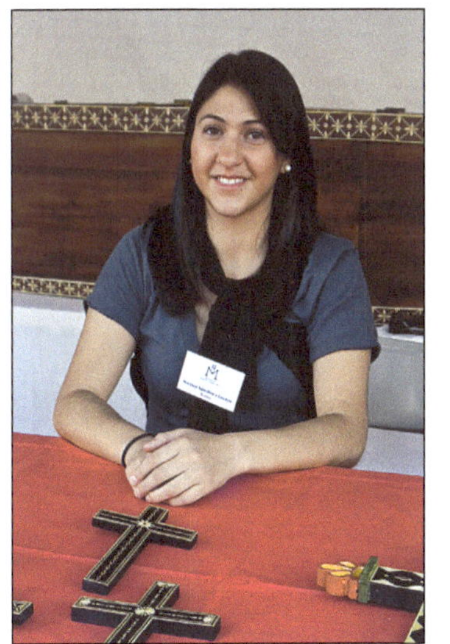

Marisol Zia Sánchez y Lucero

Art Form: Straw Appliqué
Contact: (206) 442-9795
Born in Seattle, Washington
Lives in Tome, New Mexico
Juried into Spanish Market in 2008
Notable Awards:

New Mexico Museum of International Folk Art Purchase Award.
American Institute of Art, History and Culture Best Artist Award Crafts.

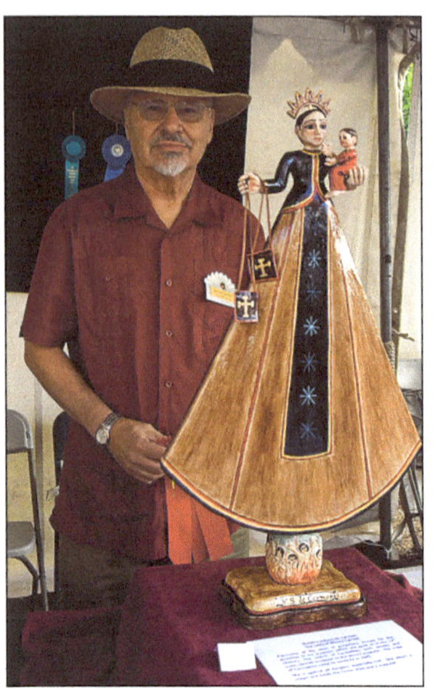

William (Art) Sánchez

Art Form: Painted *Bultos*
Contact: (505) 471-1094
Born in Clayton, New Mexico
Lives in Santa Fe, New Mexico
Juried into Spanish Market in 2008
Notable Awards:
- Spanish Market Bienvenidos Award 2008.
- New Mexico State Fair Second Place Award Hispanic Art 2006, Third Place Award Hispanic Arts 2005 and 2007.
- Española Arts Festival First Place Award Hispanic Art 2002.

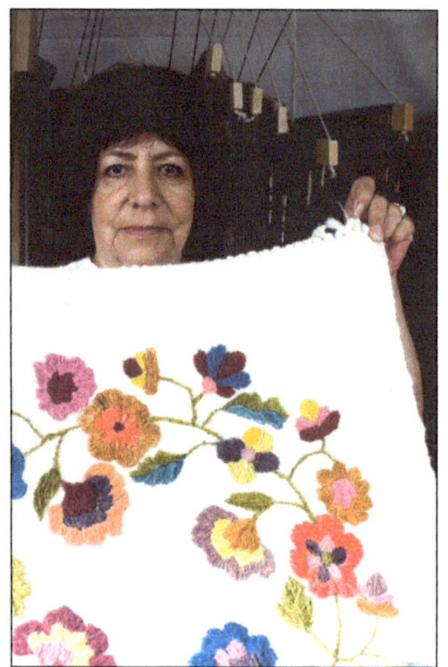

Beatrice Maestas Sandoval

Art Form(s): Colcha Embroidery, Weaving
Contact: (505) 425-8485
Born in Las Vegas, New Mexico
Lives in Las Vegas, New Mexico
Juried into Spanish Market in 1995
Notable Awards:
Spanish Market Grand Prize for Best of Show 2000.

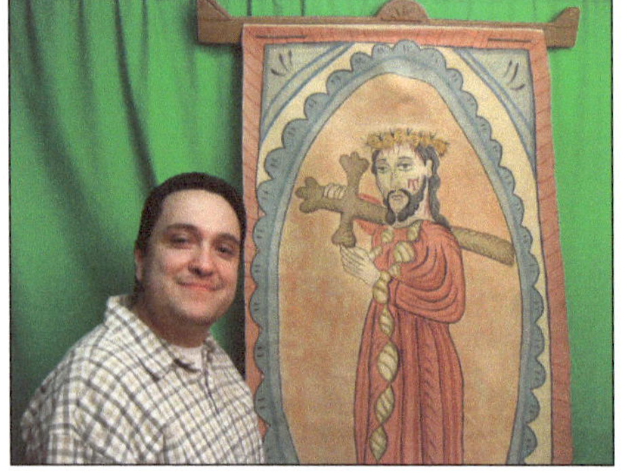

Carlos A. Santistevan, Jr.

Art Form: Hide Painting
Contact: (303) 888-1947
Born in Denver, Colorado
Lives in Denver, Colorado
Juried into Spanish Market in 2008.

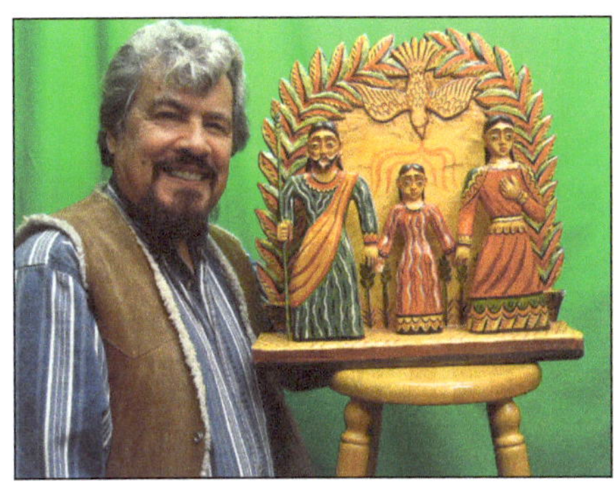

Carlos A. Santistevan, Sr.

Art Form(s): Painted *Bultos*, Altar Screens, Hide Painting
Contact: (303) 297-1370
Born in Denver, Colorado
Lives in Denver, Colorado
Juried into Spanish Market in 1978
Notable Awards:

Spanish Market Design Award 2000, Master's Award for Lifetime Achievement 2002, Boeckman and Leo Salazar Award 2005, First Place Unpainted *Bultos* and José Dolores López Award 2009.

Gregory P. Segura

Art Form: Precious Metals
Contact: (505) 670-3955
Born in Santa Fe, New Mexico
Lives in Santa Fe, New Mexico
Juried into Spanish Market in 2010
Notable Awards:
Spanish Market E Boyd Award and Second Place 2010.

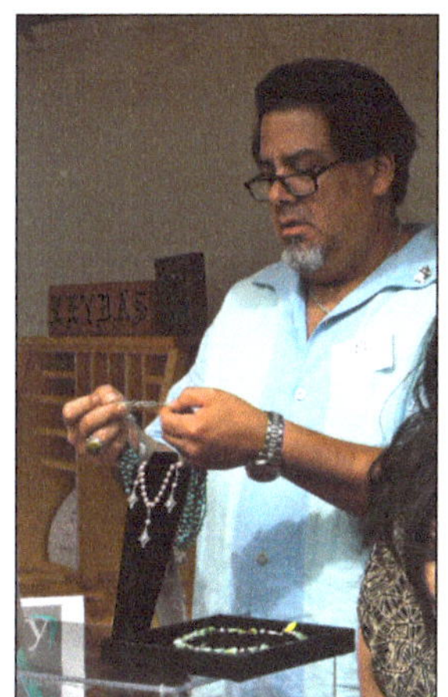

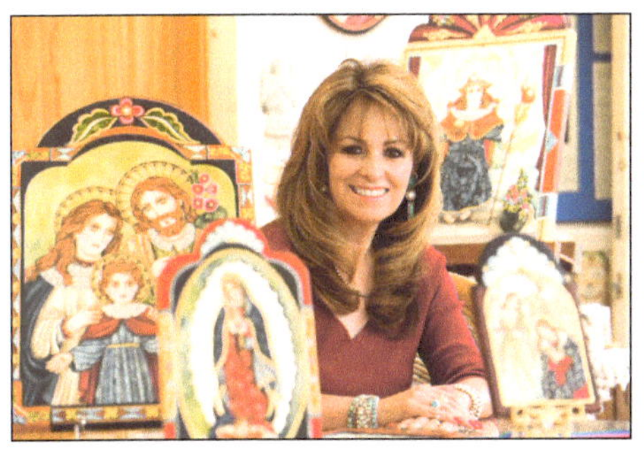

Arlene Cisneros Sena

Art Form: *Retablos*
Contact: (505) 438-0163
Born in San Luis, Colorado
Lives in Santa Fe, New Mexico
Juried into Spanish Market in 1992
Notable Awards:

Spanish Market Poster Award 1994, First Place Mixed Media 1995, Gerald Peters Award 1997, People's Choice Award 1998, Collaboration and Purchase Award 1999, Second Place Large *Retablos* and Archbishop's Award 2001, Purchase Award 2002, Second Place Large *Retablos* 2004/2006/2009, Third Place Large *Retablos* 2009.

Santa Fe Mayor's Recognition Award for Excellence in the Arts 1998.
Dual Language Education of New Mexico Poster Artist 2009.
New Mexican Hispanic Culture Preservation League Dona Eufemia Award 2010.
Governor's Award for Excellence in the Arts 2010.

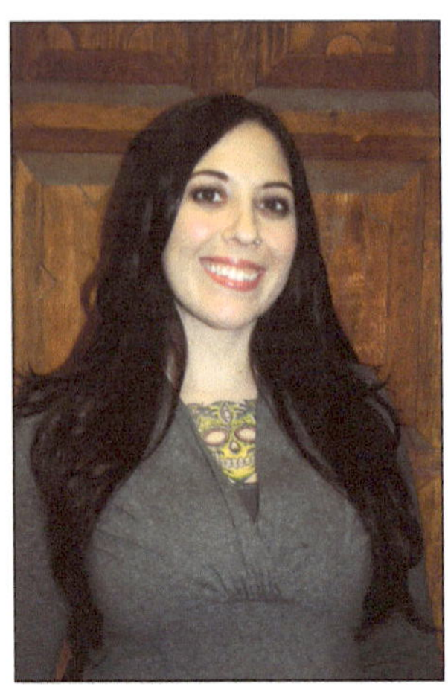

Marie Sena
Art Form: *Retablos*
Contact: 972-890-6070
Born in Santa Fe, New Mexico
Lives in Albuquerque, New Mexico
Juried into Spanish Market in 2001
Notable Awards:

Spanish Market First Place Small *Retablos* 2005 and 2006, Collaboration Award 2007, Second Place *Retablos* 2003 and 2009, Hispanic Heritage Award 2005.

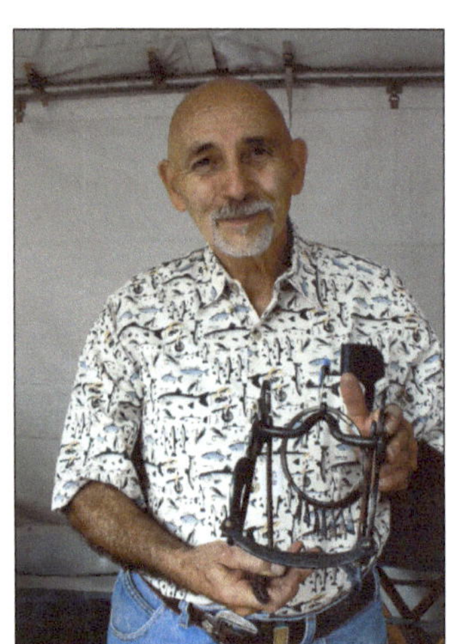

Ralph Sena
Art Form(s): Precious Metals, Ironwork
Contact: (505) 864-1816
Born in Albuquerque, New Mexico
Lives in Bosque, New Mexico
Juried into Spanish Market in 1971-73, again in 1994
Notable Awards:

Spanish Market First and Second Place Precious Metals, First Place Ironwork, Collaboration Award.
New Mexico State Fair First Place Ironwork, First Place Precious Metals, Collaboration Award.

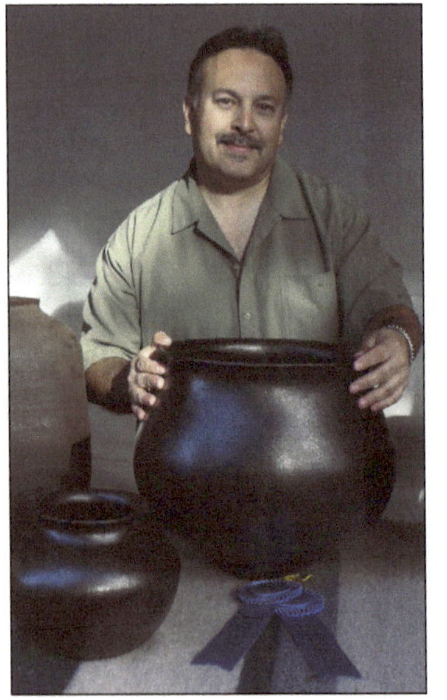

Jacobo de la Serna
Art Form(s): Painted *Bultos*, Pottery
Contact: (505) 507-6585
Born in Española, New Mexico
Lives in Albuquerque, New Mexico
Juried into Spanish Market in 1994
Notable Awards:

Spanish Market First Place Gesso Relief 1995, Purchase Award 1997 and1999, Second Place Mixed Media 1999, Utilitarian Award 2000 and 2001, Hispanic Heritage Award 2003, Distinguished Artist Award and Judges Choice Award 2000, First Place Pottery 2004/2005/2006/2007/2008/2009/2010, Second Place and Utilitarian Award 2010.
Taylor Museum Best of Show.
New Mexico Certificate of Recognition multiple years.

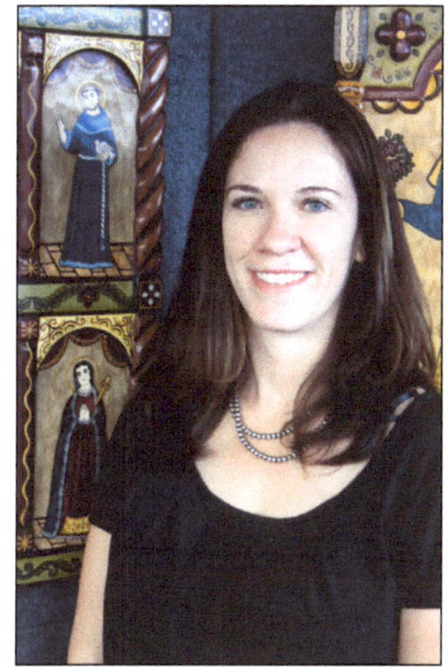

Roxanne Shaw-Galindo

Art Form: *Retablos*
Contact: (303) 258-3126
Born in Wheatridge, Colorado
Lives in Nederland, Colorado
Juried into Spanish Market in 2000
Notable Awards:
Spanish Market First Place Altar Screens 2000/2003/2010, First Place and Honorable Mention Large *Retablos* 2004, First Place Large *Retablos* 2005, José Dolores López Award 2007.

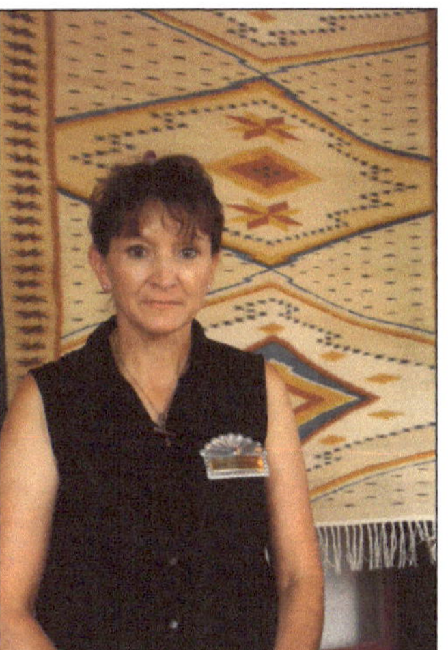

Johanna Terrazas

Art Form: Weaving
Contact: (575) 756-2907
Born in Tierra Amarilla, New Mexico
Lives in Chama, New Mexico
Juried into Spanish Market in 2000
Notable Awards:
Spanish Market Bienvenidos Award 2000, Purchase Award 2003, First and Second Place Rio Grande Weaving 2004. Cerro Mojino Woolworks Rio Grande Weaving Award 2006. New Mexico State Fair First Place and Purchase Award 2007.

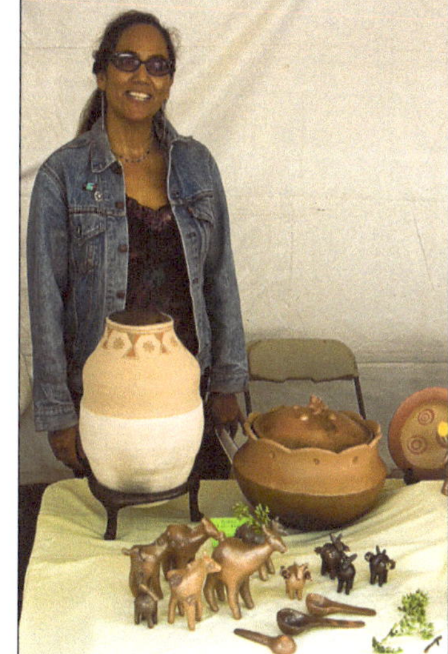

Camilla Trujillo

Art Form: Pottery
Contact: (505) 670-3271
Born in Santa Fe, New Mexico
Lives in San Pedro, New Mexico
Juried into Spanish Market in 1993
Notable Awards:
Spanish Market Heritage Award 2006, Utilitarian Award with Rene Zamora in 2007 and 2008, Collections Award 2009.

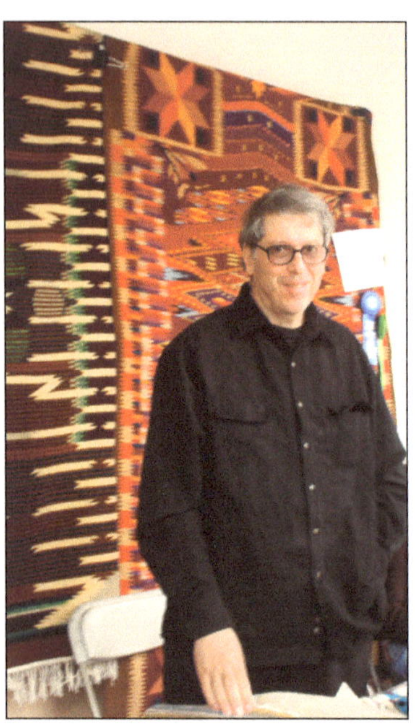

Irvin Trujillo

Art Form: Weaving
Contact: (505) 351-2180
Born in Los Alamos, New Mexico
Lives in Chimayo, New Mexico
Juried into Spanish Market in 1976
Notable Awards:
Spanish Market Grand Prize for Best of Show 1984/1991/2008.
National Endowment for the Arts National Heritage Fellowship Award.

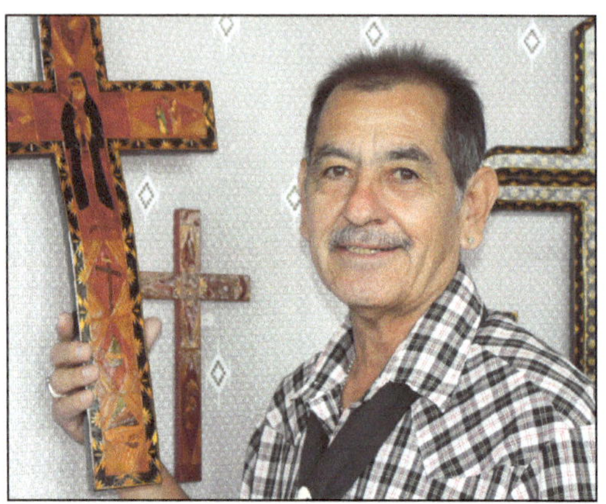

Jimmy E. Trujillo

Art Form: Straw Appliqué
Contact: (505) 842-0039
Born in Abiquiu, New Mexico
Lives in Albuquerque, New Mexico
Juried into Spanish Market in 1986
Notable Awards:
Spanish Market First Place Award 1989/1991/1993/1996/2003/2009, Purchase Award 1993, Utilitarian Award 1995, Florence Dibell Bartlett Award 1997, Hispanic Heritage Award 1998, Second Place, People's Choice and Collaboration Award 1999, Honorary Mention 2000, First Place 2003, Third Place Award 2008, Third Place and Our Lady of Guadalupe Award 2009.
New Mexico State Fair First Place 1995/2001/2004, Second Place 1996/1999/2000/2002, Honorary Mention 1996/1998/2000 and two in 2002, Third Place in 1998 and 2008.
Tesoros Foundation First in 2005/2006/2008/2009 and Best of Show 2008/2009.

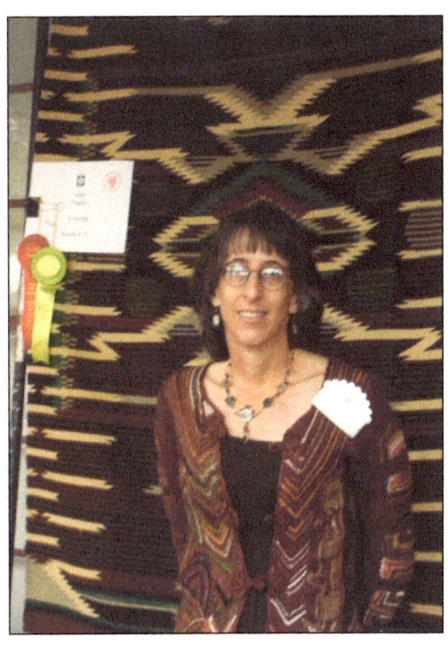

Lisa Trujillo

Art Form: Weaving
Contact: (505) 351-2180
Born in San Diego, California
Lives in Chimayo, New Mexico
Juried into Spanish Market in 1982
Notable Awards:

Spanish Market Awards for Rio Grande Weaving 1986/1987/1996, Jake O. Trujillo Award 1997/1998/2003/2004, La Lana Weaving Award 1998/1999/2010, Second Place 2002 and 2005, First Place 2003, Second Place Excellence in Rio Grande Weaving 2010.

Lucy Trujillo

Art Form: Weaving
Contact: (505) 351-4534
Born in Rio Chiquito, New Mexico
Lives in Chimayo, New Mexico
Juried into Spanish Market in 2006
Notable Awards:
Rio Grande Sun Recognition 2007 and 2010.

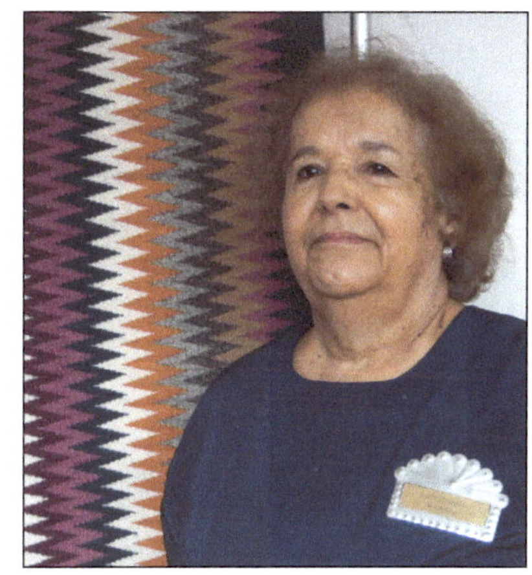

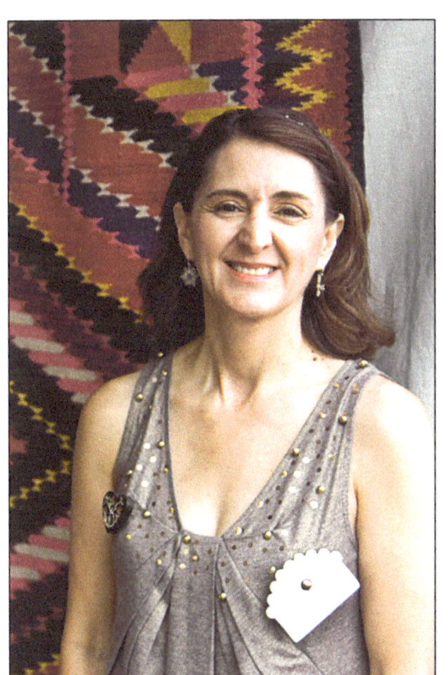

Della Vigil Ulibarri

Art Form: Straw Appliqué
Contact: (505) 471-8699
Born in Española, New Mexico
Lives in Santa Fe, New Mexico
Juried into Spanish Market in 2008
Notable Awards:

Santa Fe County Fair First Place Traditional Art Category and Best of Show 2008.

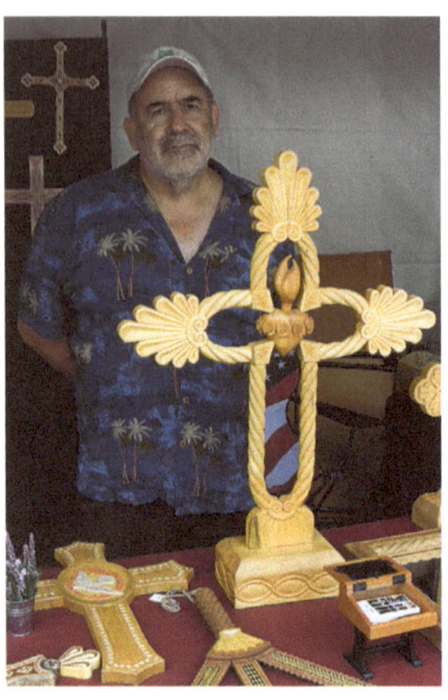

Lee J. Valdez

Art Form: Woodcarving
Contact: (505) 753-9841
Born in Santa Cruz, New Mexico
Lives in Española, New Mexico
Juried into Spanish Market in 2002
Notable Awards:

Spanish Market Bienvenidos Award 2002, First Place 2009.
New Mexico State Fair Second Place 2000/2001/2002/2007/2008/2010,
Santos of New Mexico Award 2003, First Place and Third Place 2004 and 2005,
De Colores Award 2004 and 2006.
Picuris Pueblo Art Show Best of Show 2003.
Española Valley Arts Festival First Place Furniture 2004.
Grants Fiesta de Colores Third Place 2006, Second Place 2010.

Timothy Valdez

Art Form: Straw Appliqué
Contact: (505) 470-0011
Born in Santa Fe, New Mexico
Lives in Santa Fe, New Mexico
Juried into Spanish Market in 1985
Notable Awards:

Spanish Market People's Choice Award,
Honorable Mention, Archbishop's Award,
Diane Besser Award.
New Mexico State Fair three
Third Place Awards.

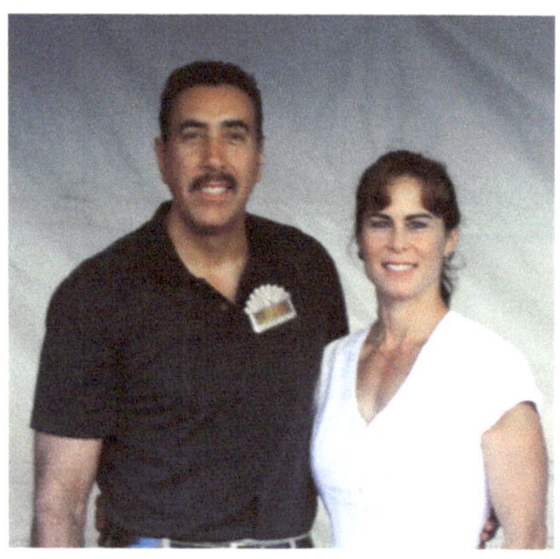

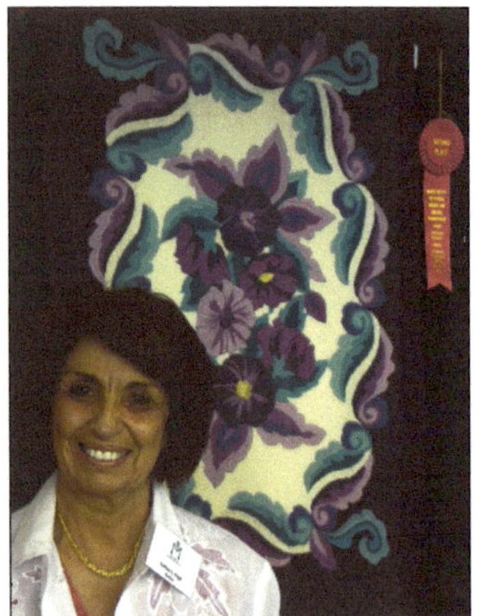

Esther L. Vigil

Art Form: Colcha Embroidery
Contact: (505) 822-8907
Born in Española, New Mexico
Lives in Albuquerque, New Mexico
Juried into Spanish Market in 2010
Notable Awards:

Spanish Market Second Place 2010.

Eugene Vigil

Art Form: Weaving
Contact: (505) 351-4522
Born in Española, New Mexico
Lives in Chimayo, New Mexico
Juried into Spanish Market in 1995
Notable Awards:
Taos Wool Festival Silver Medallion 2009.
Tesoro Cultural Center Best of Show 2010.

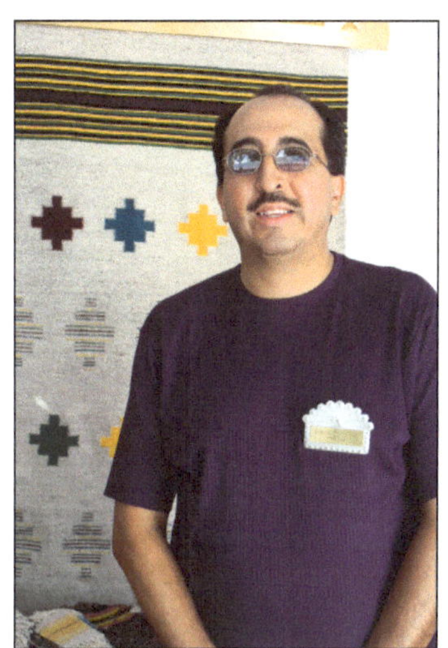

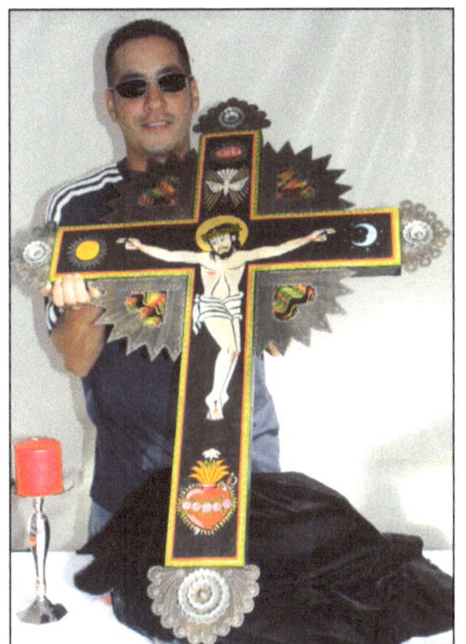

Gabriel James Vigil

Art Form: *Retablos*
Contact: (505) 577-4113
Born in Raton, New Mexico
Lives in Santa Fe, New Mexico
Juried into Spanish Market in 1995
Notable Awards:
Spanish Market First Place Small *Retablos* 2004, Second Place Small *Retablos* 2005 and 2006, Honorable Mention Small *Retablos* 2007, Poster Award 2008, Winter Market People's Choice Award 2009.

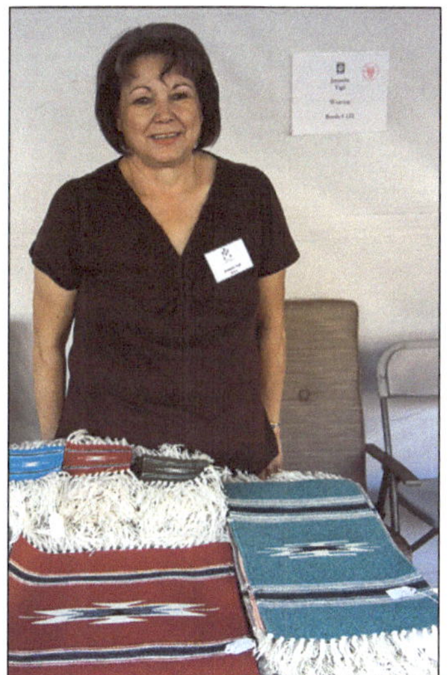

Jennette Vigil

Art Form: Weaving
Contact: (505) 689-2307
Born in Embudo, New Mexico
Lives in Ojo Sarco, New Mexico
Juried into Spanish Market in 1990.

Marie E. Vigil

Art Form: Weaving
Contact: (505) 351-4806
Born in Rio Chiquito, New Mexico
Lives in Cundiyo, New Mexico
Juried into Spanish Market in 2000
Notable Awards:
Northern New Mexico Community College Show
Honorable Mention Award 1999.

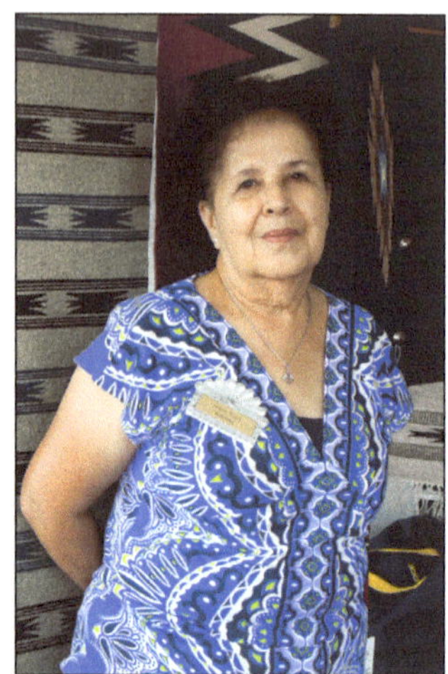

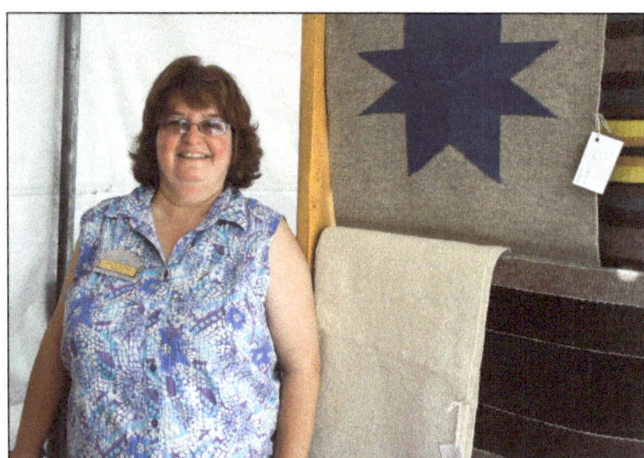

Rose A. Vigil

Art Form: Weaving
Contact: (505) 351-4522
Born in Española, New Mexico
Lives in Chimayo, New Mexico
Juried into Spanish Market in 1995
Notable Awards:

Spanish Market Second Place Award for Excellence in Rio Grande Textiles and Jake O. Trujillo Award 2009,
Third Place Award for Excellence in Rio Grande Textiles 2010.
Taos Wool Festival Silver Medal 2010.

Nina Arroyo Wood

Art Form: Colcha Embroidery
Lives in Santa Fe, New Mexico
Juried into Spanish Market in 2003.

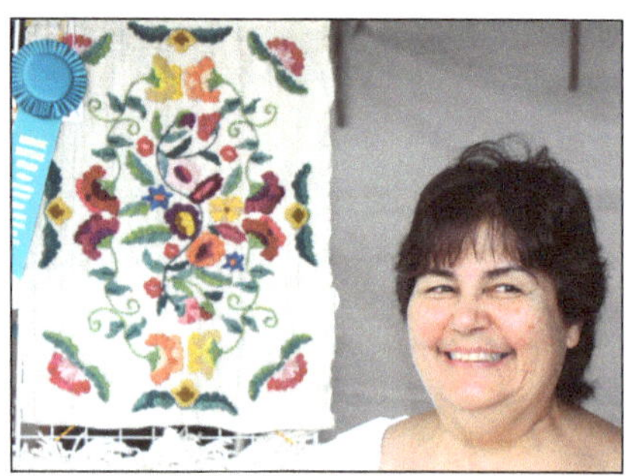

Jason Younis y Delgado
Art Form: Tinwork
Contact: (505) 385-3525
Born in Can Tho, Viet Nam
Lives in Albuquerque, New Mexico
Juried into Spanish Market in 1989.

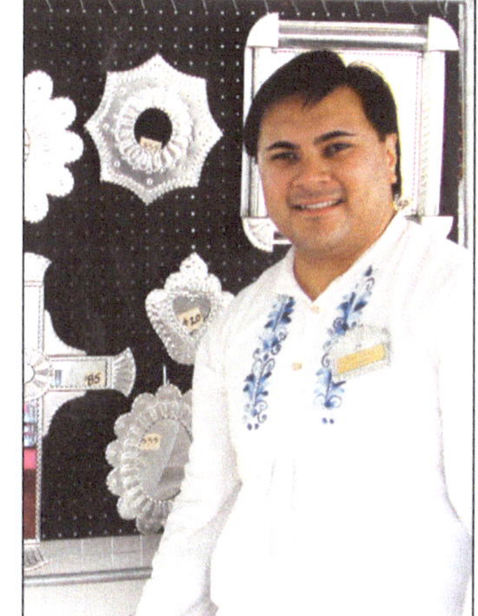

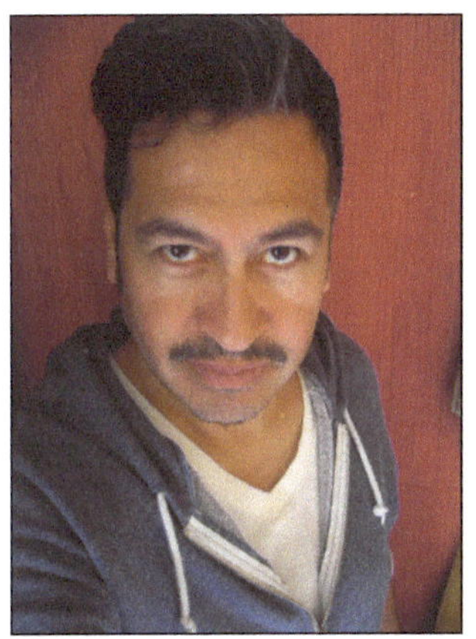

Frank Zamora
Art Form: *Retablos*
Contact: (303) 287-5637
Born in Denver, Colorado
Lives in Commerce City, Colorado
Juried into Spanish Market in 2008
Notable Awards:
Spanish Market Third Place Large *Retablos* 2008,
Poster Award 2009,
New Directions Award 2010.

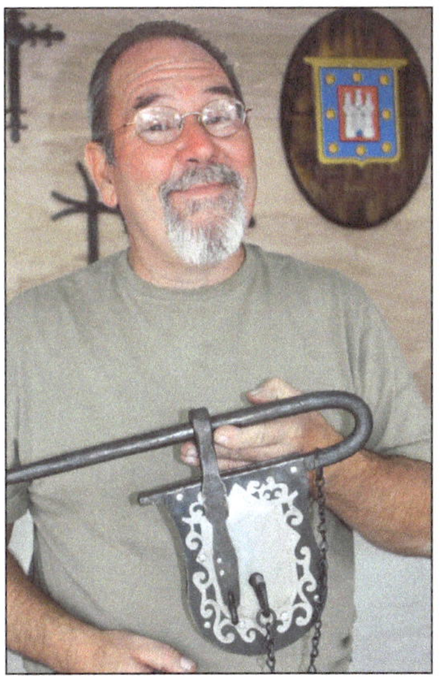

René Zamora
Art Form: Ironwork
Contact: (505) 795-8848
Born in Santa Fe, New Mexico
Lives in Santa Fe, New Mexico
Juried into Spanish Market in 2002
Notable Awards:
Spanish Market Honorable Mention 2002,
Second Place and Purchase Award 2003, First Place 2004,
Utilitarian Award, 2007 and 2008, Collaboration Award with Camilla Trujillo 2007/2008/2009,
Collections Committee Award 2009,
Ironwork Award 2010.

In the mid 1960s, the Society established a Grand Prize (Best of Show) Award. Awardees are listed below.

SPANISH MARKET GRAND PRIZE (BEST OF SHOW) AWARDEES

2010 Julia R. Gómez (*Colcha* Embroidery)
2009 Andrew Garcia (Furniture)
2008 Irvin L. Trujillo (Weaving)
2007 Kathleen Sais Lerner (*Colcha* Embroidery)
2006 Irvin L. Trujillo (Weaving)
2005 Martha Vároz Ewing (Straw Appliqué)
2004 Alcario Otero (*Bultos*)
2003 Alcario Otero (Gesso and Wood Relief)
2002 Federico Prudencio (Furniture)
2001 Yolanda Griego (Straw Appliqué)
2000 Beatrice Maestas Sandoval (*Colcha* Embroidery)
1999 Karen Martinez (Weaving)
1998 Felix López (Painted *Bultos*)
1997 David Nabor Lucero (Painted *Bultos)*
1996 David Nabor Lucero (Painted *Bultos*)
1995 Alcario Otero (*Reredos*)
1994 Gustavo Victor Goler (Painted *Bultos*)
1993 Ramón José López (Furniture)
1992 Gustavo Victor Goler (Painted *Bultos*)
1991 Irvin Trujillo (Weaving)
1990 Charlie Carrillo (Painted *Bultos*)
1989 Ramón José López (Altar screen)
1988 Marie Romero Cash (Painted *Bultos*)

1987 Marie Romero Cash (Painted *Bultos*)
1986 Jake Trujillo (Weaving)
1985 Anita Romero Jones (Tin Altar Screen with Hide Painting)
1984 Irvin Trujillo (Weaving)
1983 Ramón José López (Spanish Colonial Silver-Holloware)
1982 Jake Trujillo (Weaving)
1981 Eliseo Rodriguez (Straw Appliqué)
1980 María Lujan (*Colcha* Embroidery)
1979 David C. de Baca (Furniture)
1978 Teresa Archuleta Sagel (Weaving)
1977 María Vergara Wilson (Weaving)
1976 Gloria López Córdova (Woodcarving)
1975 (No Grand Prize Given)
1974 Unknown
1973 Unknown
1972 Unknown
1971 María Lujan (*Colcha* Embroidery)
1970 María Lujan (*Colcha* Embroidery)
1969 Apolonio Mártinez (Woodcarving)
1968 Unknown
1967 Unknown
1966 (No Market)
1965 Ben Ortega (Woodcarving)

The only pre-selected award at Spanish Market is the Master's Award for Lifetime Achievement. This Award was inaugurated in 1987 and was first sponsored by the *Feria Artesana* of Albuquerque from 1988 to 1991 and then sponsored by KASA Fox 2 from 1992 to 2006. The Award is now sponsored by the Spanish Colonial Arts Society in honor of an artist who meets specific criteria:

The artist has received awards at Spanish Market and at other festivals/fairs/exhibitions.

The artist has given back to the community as a teacher, and improved the image of the art form.

The artist is included in private and museum collections.

The artist has raised awareness of the art form on a regional and/or national level.

Recipient must have participated at least 15 years in Spanish Market and be currently exhibiting.

The Awardees are listed below.

MASTERS AWARD FOR LIFETIME ACHIEVEMENT

2010 Belarmino Esquibel (*Retablos*)
2009 Gloria López Córdova (Woodcarving)
2008 Ramón José López (*Bultos*, Furniture, Hide Painting, Precious Metals, *Retablos*)
2007 Félix A. López (Santos)
2006 Charles M. Carrillo (Santos)
2005 Irvin Trujillo (Weaving)
2004 John Jiménez (*Retablos*)
2003 David C. de Baca (Furniture)
2002 Carlos Santisteven, Sr. (Santos)
2001 Cordelia Coronado and Eppie Archuleta (Weaving)

2000 Sabinita López Ortiz (Córdova Woodcarving)
1999 Bonifacio Sandoval (Tinwork)
1998 Eulogio and Zoraida Ortega (Santos and Weaving)
1997 Ricardo López (Córdova Woodcarving)
1996 Frank Brito (Woodcarving)
1995 Ben Ortega (Woodcarving)
1994 Monica Sosaya Halford (Santos and *Colcha* Embroidery)
1993 Tomás L. Sena (Woodcarving)
1992 Marie Romero Cash (Santos)
1991 Angelina Delgado Mártinez (Tinwork)
1990 Leo George Salazar (Woodcarving)
1989 Eliseo and Paula Rodriguez (Straw Appliqué)
1988 Emilio and Senaida Romero (Tinwork)
1987 Horacio Valdez (Santos)

Museum of Spanish Colonial Art

By the early 1950s, the Society Board expressed their desire for a permanent museum to house and exhibit the growing art collection, which then consisted of several hundred pieces. The Board knew that a museum to store and showcase the collection would allow them to further their mission, which included educating the public about the art forms. Because the collection was safeguarded in the homes of Society members, there were storage and security concerns.

In 1938, the Society arranged with the Palace of the Governors to mount an exhibition of 48 Society art pieces at the Palace, which was the first significant exhibit of art from the collection. The New Mexico International Folk Art Museum was completed in 1953 and later graciously agreed to store the collection for the Society, until such time as the Society could build a museum to house the collections. E Boyd served as curator of both the New Mexico International Folk Art Museum and the Spanish Colonial Arts Society during this time and she was instrumental in setting up this storage arrangement.

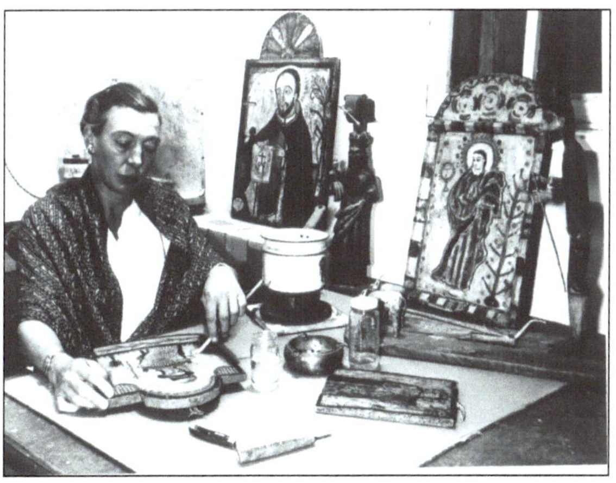

E Boyd in her studio

Ruth Catlin of Santa Fe donated land in 1961 that she hoped could some day be the site of a museum for the collection. After careful consideration, the Board decided that the location of the land was not conducive to a museum site and the land was later sold, forming the first significant funding for the proposed museum. In 1989, Alan and Ann Vedder both died within a few months of one another, and they not only left their collection to the Society but each left a significant donation with the intent that the funds be used to build a museum. The Board believed that these gifts set the stage for a Capital Campaign to build a permanent home for the collection.

On May 17, 1998, the Society received an anonymous gift of 2.6 acres of land and a historic residence to be used as core gallery space of a proposed museum. The original 5000-square-foot residence that was gifted to the Society was commissioned and financed by John D. Rockefeller, Jr. for use by the Center for Anthropological Studies, and was designed by John Gaw Meem in 1930. The building is a wonderful example of the "Spanish Colonial" style for which Meem is known, and the building provides an intimate setting for visitors to view the collection and other exhibit items. Meem had been involved with the Society from its incorporation and he and his wife, Faith, were active members and supporters. They donated a substantial gift of 147 *bultos* and *retablos* to the Society collection in 1985.

Eileen Wells and Barbara Carpio Hoover agreed to chair the Capital Campaign to raise funds for the restoration of the residence to adapt it for museum use, and the design and construction of an attached 8000-square-foot collection storage building. The campaign was launched in the summer of 1999 and many generous donors stepped forward to make the long-held dream of a Spanish Colonial art museum a reality. The largest foundation gifts were received from: The Brown Foundation, The Santa Fe Community Foundation, the Edgar Foster Daniels Foundation, The Kresge Foundation, The Fondren Foundation, The M.A. Healy Foundation, The LLWW Foundation, the Hale Matthews Foundation, The

Stockman Family Foundation, and the Eugene V. and Clare E. Thaw Charitable Trust. Many additional gifts of various amounts were also received from individual donors.

The Museum of Spanish Colonial Art opened to the public in July, 2002, becoming the only museum in the world dedicated to Spanish Colonial art, with a special focus on the unique art styles developed in New Mexico. There are more than 3500 unique art objects in the collection and the museum is an important research facility as well as exhibit space.

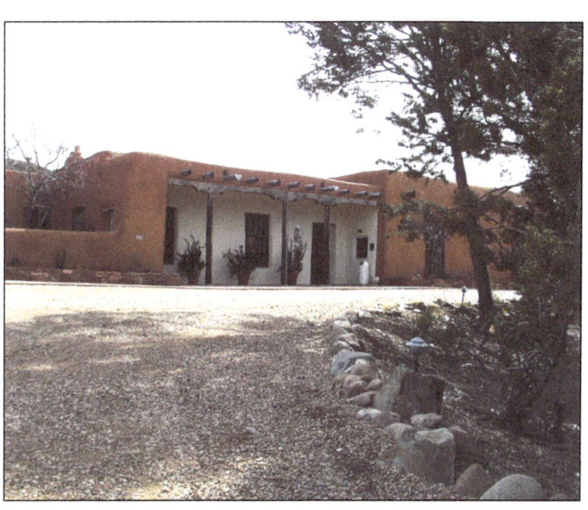

Museum of Spanish Colonial Art

During the 1990s, the focus of collecting shifted to art created in the 20th century and many pieces have been purchased from current Spanish Market award-winning artists. Donations of quality art are frequently given to the Society and the collection continues to grow. Sixty-three art objects from the collection are featured in two major exhibits about Spanish life at the Palace of the Governors.

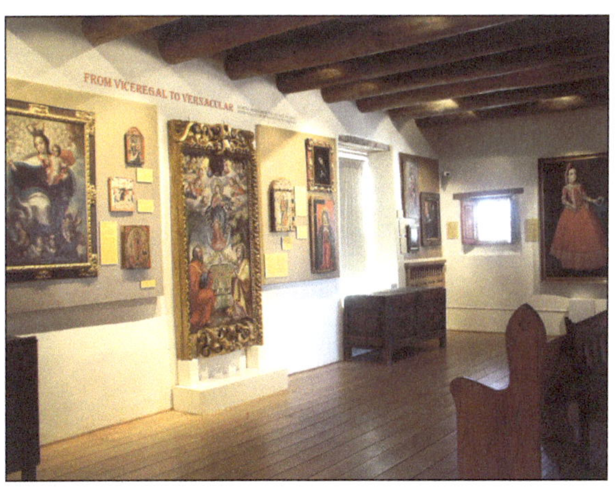

Wall of Viceregal to Vernacular Exhibit

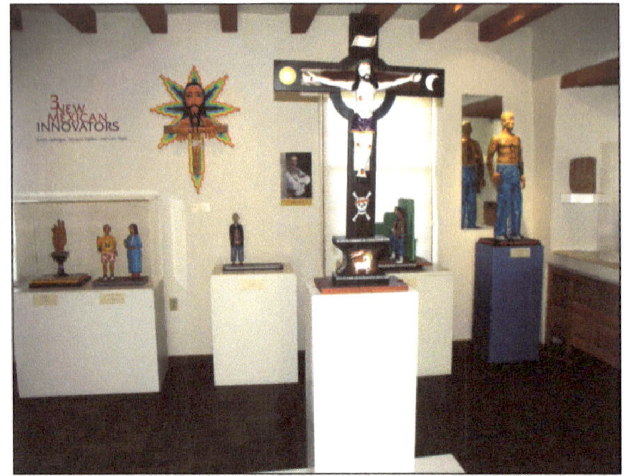

View of Three New Mexican Innovators Exhibit

Robin Farwell Gavin replaced Donna Pierce as Senior Curator in May, 2003, and continues to mount exciting, educational art exhibits drawn from the collection and borrowed from around the world. More than thirty-one exhibits have been mounted since the opening of the museum, ranging from one-gallery shows to exhibits filling the entire museum. The Museum of Spanish Colonial Art stands as a testament to the 86-year commitment of local men and women who believed that the traditional arts descended from the Spanish Colonial influence are worth preserving and promoting. The museum is the only one of its kind in the world, and continues to attract the support of those who believe this heritage deserves preservation.

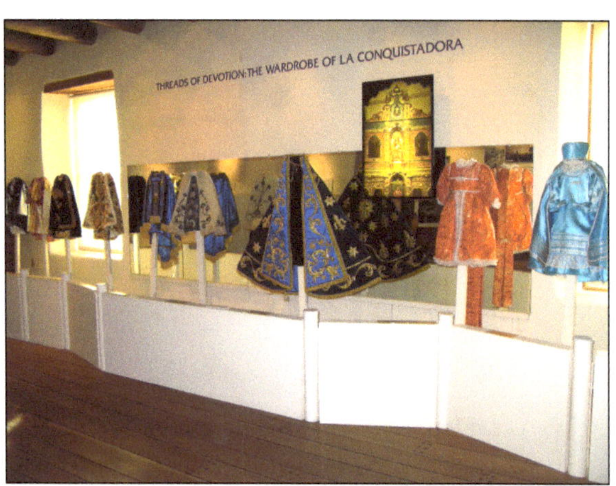

La Conquistadora Exhibit

Museum of Spanish Colonial Art Exhibition History

Ongoing

Recent Acquisitions. Ongoing changing exhibits highlighting recent additions to the collections.

Delgado Room. Depicting typical main room of weathly Spaniard living in New Mexico in 1815, details taken from last will of Captain Manuel Delgado.

2011

Collecting New Mexico—E Boyd. A look at the first scholar of New Mexican colonial art and first curator of the Spanish Colonial Arts Society and how she shaped our view of New Mexico's past. January 2012.

Collecting New Mexico: The Forgotten Cady Wells. Exhibit explores the impact that modernist artist Cady Wells had on the collection and study of New Mexican colonial art and how this art affected his painting. January–December, 2011.

2010

Threads of Devotion: The Wardrobe of La Conquistadora. The first museum exhibition of some of the clothing made for the oldest and most revered image of the Virgin Mary in New Mexico. The exhibit discusses the history of the image and the tradition of clothing images throughout the Catholic world. September–December, 2010.

Spanish Market Gallery. Exhibit of the work of some of today's accomplished Spanish Market Artists.

Women in New Mexico: Concha Ortiz y Pino de Kleven (1910–2006). Explored the life of the first female majority whip of a State legislature in the country and her legacy for New Mexico. For Women's History Month.

2009

Converging Streams: Art of the Hispanic and Native American Southwest (with William Wroth, guest curator). A groundbreaking exhibition examining the cross-cultural influences between Native American and Hispanic artistic technique, design, and aesthetic.

New Mexican Embroidery: Tradition and Innovation (with Josie Caruso, guest curator). New information concerning the history, use, and production of embroidery in New Mexico.

2008

Straw Appliqué: A Poor Man's Gold (with Helen Lucero, guest curator). A selection of historic and contemporary pieces illustrating the design and technique of this traditional art form.

Three New Mexican Innovators: Celso Gallegos, Luis Tapia, and Horacio Valdez (with Helen Lucero, guest curator). A look at three of New Mexico's artists and how they impacted the traditional arts.

2007

Sitting Pretty: Seating in 19th Century New Mexico. A selection of stools, side chairs, and arm chairs from the museum's collection illustrating changes in use and in style from ca. 1750–1900. October 26, 2007–June 2008.

Félix López: Master Santero, featuring selected works by the artist and his son, Joseph, and daughter, Krissa. June–October, 2007.

2006

From Viceregal to Vernacular: Painting in Colonial Mexico and New Mexico. Featuring selected works from the Jan and Frederick Mayer Collection at the Denver Art Museum. An exhibition of Mexican colonial portraits and religious paintings compared with New Mexican *retablos*.

The Art of Spanish Market, 1965–2005. A survey of art produced by modern day artists working with traditional art forms and techniques, and the changes that have occurred in their work over the last 40 years.

***Relicarios*: Devotional Miniatures from the Americas.** Exhibition of 78 *relicarios* on loan from a private collection with a discussion of their use and symbolism.

2005

***La Granada*: the Pomegranate in New Spain.** History and symbolism of the pomegranate in Spain and in Spanish Colonial art, including furniture, textiles, ceramics, and metalwork.

Río Grande Weaving: the H. P. Mera Collection. An examination of the different styles of weaving introduced by the Spanish into New Mexico and how they incorporated and influenced Native American textiles.

2004

A Tapestry of Kinship: Rediscovered *Santeros* of Colonial Santa Fe. Exhibition introducing the groundbreaking academic work of guest curators Charles M. Carrillo, PhD, and José Antonio Esquibel regarding the identity of Santa Fe's colonial artists.

2003/2004

***El Brillo de la Plata*/The Shimmer of Silver.** Spanish Colonial and contemporary silver in New México.

2003

***El Retablo Nuevomexicano*/The New Mexican *Retablo*.** Discussion of the stylistic development of the *retablo* in colonial and 19th century New Mexico.

2002

***Conexiones*: Connections in Spanish Colonial Art.** Inaugural exhibition for the new Museum of Spanish Colonial Art exploring the relationship of the art of New Mexico with the rest of the colonial world. Curator: Donna Pierce.

San Ysidro Labrador. A look at the many images of this saint from different countries. Curator: Donna Pierce.

Index

www.ingramcontent.com/pod-product-compliance
Lightning Source LLC
LaVergne TN
LVHW070216110826
845147LV00003B/581
9780865348219